25TH ANNIVERSARY EDITION

On Writing
the College
Application
ESSAY

On Writing the College Application ESSAY

The Key to Acceptance at the College of Your Choice

HARRY BAULD

COLLINS REFERENCE
An Imprint of HarperCollins Publishers
www.harpercollins.com

ON WRITING THE COLLEGE APPLICATION ESSAY. Copyright © 1987, 2012 by Harold J. Bauld. All rights reserved. Printed in the United States of America. No part of this book may be used or reproduced in any manner whatsoever without written permission except in the case of brief quotations embodied in critical articles and reviews. For information, address HarperCollins Publishers, Inc., 10 East 53rd Street, New York, N.Y. 10022.

HarperCollins books may be purchased for educational, business, or sales promotional use. For information, please write: Special Markets Department, HarperCollins Publishers, 10 East 53rd Street, New York, NY 10022.

First published in 1987 by Harper & Row Publishers.

This twenty-fifth anniversary edition published in 2012 by Collins Reference.

Grateful acknowledgment is made for permission to reprint the following:

"Summer Beyond Wish" by Russell Baker. Copyright © 1978 by The New York Times Company. Reprinted by permission.

"A Failure of Faith in Man-Made Things" from *Close to Home* by Ellen Goodman. © 1986, *The Boston Globe* Newspaper, Washington Post Writers Group. Reprinted with permission.

"Pfft" by David Owen. © 1986 by David Owen, Reprinted from *The Atlantic Monthly*, December 1986.

"Beer Can" by John Updike. © 1964 by John Updike. Reprinted from *Assorted Prose* by John Updike, by permission of Alfred A. Knopf, Inc. Originally appeared in *The New Yorker*.

Excerpt from "Heavier Than Air" in *Poems and Sketches of E. B. White*. Copyright © 1952 by E. B. White. Reprinted by permission of Harper & Row Publishers, Inc.

The Library of Congress has cataloged a previous edition as follows:

Bauld, Harry.
     On writing the college application essay.
     1. College applications. ' 2. Exposition (Rhetoric). 3. Universities and colleges—Admission. I. Title.
LB2351.5.B38   1987   378'.1057   86-46043
ISBN 0-06-055076-7 (hc)   ISBN 978-0-06-463722-0 (pbk.)
ISBN 0-06-463722-0 (pbk.)

ISBN 978-0-06-212399-2

12   13   14   15   16   DIX/RRD   10   9   8   7   6   5   4   3   2   1

For Lizzy, Molly,
Xabier, and my students

And because I found I had nothing else to write about,
I presented myself as a subject.

Montaigne

Contents

Acknowledgments

Since its publication in a previous century this book has picked up a happy trail of debt that begins with the original cast (Bill Oliver, Jim Rogers, Jim McMenamin, Beth Janes, Kristin Crowley, Sally Goldfarb, Nathan and the late Betty Straus, Marti Straus, Gary and Eleanor Cornog, Jane and Ben Momo, the late Ursula Cino, Steve Bauld, Marian Young, Jeanne Flagg) and continues with appreciation that is ongoing to Jerry Kisslinger, Chris Daly, Anne Fishel, Larry Momo, Irv Schenkler, Mike Lacopo, David Schiller, and the Nat Sobel Agency.

Among a number of people who have had a material impact on the life of this book since the first edition are Steven Singer, Cathy Nabbefeld, Hugh Silbaugh, and Joyce Vining Morgan.

My gratitude is great to the faculty, staff, and trustees of the Putney School. One of the most noble and intense places on earth, Putney is not so much a school as an unforgettable blast of life-altering voltage. Many thanks to all my friends and former colleagues there.

I bow to everyone at Horace Mann School in New York, where I began the work of this book and to which I have happily returned after many years away.

Inés Gómez-Ochoa has been an inspiration in every possible way.

My greatest debt is certainly to the Putney and Horace Mann students I taught and who, it is no tepid cliché to say, have taught me for nearly thirty years. The writing of many of them appears in the book with their permission: Iymaani Abdul-Hamid, Rani Arbo, Gideon Broshy, Caitlin Cohen, Roland Davis, Lori Dershowitz, Gerard Greweldinger, Carlyn Grose, Jennifer Gross, Sabrina Hahn, Sharon Isaak, Justine Klineman, Sean Lanigan, Philip Lee, Evin Luehrs, Nicole Parisier, Ghita Schwarz, Rebecca Segall, Rebecca Shannon, Melanie Berger Turek, and Meredith Wollins Paley. Chris Axline and John Bailo have also kindly granted permission to reprint their essays.

Preface to the Twenty-Fifth Anniversary Edition

When I finished the first edition of this book in 1986, Columbia University, which had gone coed only three years before, boasted its lowest admission rate ever: 30 percent. That year Harvard University, then as now the most selective college in the country, accepted a scant 17 percent of all applicants. The competition to be admitted to these and other Ivy League schools was described in the press of the time as "fierce," "cutthroat," and "brutal."

In 2011, Bowdoin College, which doesn't even require the SAT, admitted 15.6 percent of its applicants. Columbia accepted 6.9 percent; Harvard, 6.2 percent.

In 1986 the Common Application was itself a teenager—only 114 colleges accepted it, none of them Ivy League schools. In 2011–12, 456 colleges used it, including all of the Ivies.

In 1986, the Internet, which contained almost nothing, was known only to a handful of academics and computer geeks. Colleges urged applicants to type (remember *paper?*), though even handwriting was acceptable; at Brown University in the early 1980s we *required* the essay be handwritten, for that human touch. In 2011–12, almost everyone applies online.

The SAT since the mid-1980s has changed its name and added—of all things—an essay!

In 1986 students typically applied to six or seven schools. Now applying to twelve to fifteen schools is routine, and many students apply to more.

Since the first edition of this book, Harvard gave up its Early Action program for a couple of years and then changed its mind and reinstituted it.

Don't get me started on vinyl record albums and rotary dial telephones with cords. . . .

In this brave new world, some of the rigging of the original edition of *On Writing the College Application Essay,* which has bobbed along atop the waves of these changes for more than twenty years, has inevitably gotten a little weather-beaten.

But the new climate means the essay has become even more important, and this edition has been refitted to be more shipshape in the current admissions, um, currents.

I've cut material that seems no longer helpful and added parts based on more than twenty years of consulting schools and working with thousands of students.

There's a new chapter specifically devoted to supplements, and there's a chapter of recent student essays with my commentary to serve as examples and inspirations.

I've rewritten the entire chapter titled "The Gray Area" to bring it up to date, and I've done a revision of some kind on almost every page of the rest of the book, adding information and techniques that students have found beneficial, while (I hope) retaining the parts and character that have made the book useful for so long.

I've shortened the anthology of professional pieces because so much is now easily available on the Internet, though I wanted to retain at least a few examples to hand.

I haven't updated every reference, though. Perhaps out of nostalgia and affection for a simpler time, I have left in some examples from the first edition that clearly take place, as the current phrase has it, "back in the day." Since the book first came out I've been surprised and gratified that it has been used not only for admissions purposes and in college counseling offices but also in English classrooms around the country as a writing guide. This suggests to me that even though a number of these essays sometimes refer to comically ancient history such as the Beatles, VCRs, and centuries that begin with the number 19, much of the student writing is if not timeless then still excellent and relevant in its essentials. The bathroom essay, for example, seems ripped from today's headlines.

So in spite of the dismal statistics cited every year in the press—and I sometimes wonder, from the colleges' gleeful celebration of single-digit acceptance rates, if the ultimate admissions goal is to be so selective as to take no one at all—the essence of what you need to do on a college acceptance essay remains even more intensely the same: be your best self, clearly, concisely, and entertainingly.

Introduction

O n a fall day not long ago I returned to the high school where I once taught English, to "address the senior class." (In the past I simply talked to students, but it seems any time you travel more than 150 miles to say something you are entitled to a lot more respect.)

The place was packed; even students who had cut my classes were there, looking angelic and attentive. There was a reason for that, I knew. My subject was College Admissions.

I hadn't even finished panting from the four-flight trudge up to the auditorium before a girl stood up in the middle of the crowd and asked The Question.

"What are they looking for on those application essays, anyway?"

Faced with that same query hundreds of times I've always been tempted to mimic the Zen master who, when asked "What is Zen?" by his students, simply put his slippers on his head and left the room. But Western sympathy has prevailed and I've stayed behind with my shoes on, trying to explain why "What are they looking for?"—like "What's going to be on the test?"—is an Unquestion, or at least the wrong question.

This book will help you ask (and answer) the right questions. There are two reasons for you to concentrate on your essay. Number One you may already be intimately acquainted with: it's not easy. In fact, it's a pain in at least two anatomical areas. As an admissions officer, I've seen the doom and dismay in the faces of thousands of applicants who've asked me about the essay, and as a teacher I've watched my students agonize over them. (Once, in the dark backward and abysm of time, I even wrote a couple of college essays myself.) So I know it's the hardest part of applying, even more grinding than the SAT, which at least *ends* after three hours. Finishing an essay seems to take forever, and there are always more interesting things to do, like putting sharp sticks in your eyes.

But the second reason to concentrate on it is a happy one. The essay can be your ticket out of the faceless applicant hordes and into First Choice University. And unlike everything else in your application—the grades, recommendations, and tests, which are by now out of your hands—you have real control over your writing, right up to the last frantic minute. Essays show the admissions committee who you are, and it's your chance to let fly, uninterrupted.

You may be more frightened than excited by that opportunity. Many of my students, facing the task at first, have shrugged and said, "I speak better than I write. I'll concentrate on the interview." But, as you'll see in chapter one, pinning your hopes on the interview is not a good idea.

My students' doubts about themselves were reflected in the advice of some adults I talked to when I began this book, who suggested I'd have to write "down" toward some Common Denominator. The way they described it, this Common Denominator must have one set of knuckles wrapped around a blunt Crayola and the other dragging on the ground.

But I don't believe I have to write down. Even though we're all swamped every day with sloppy and deceitful language and bad writing, you can learn to say something simple and meaningful—and that's all a college essay asks. Just as my students did, you can write a good one that distinguishes you from everybody else. What nobody can do is just "dash it off." In fact, before you even put pen to application there are two things you must do to help yourself:

1. *Read other essays.* Familiarity breeds knowledge. Every writer working in a special form—sonnet, mystery novel, diet book, college essay—needs to know how it has been handled in the past, the good and the bad. Being able to navigate the shoals of cliché and convention is a necessity for the sailor in college-essay waters. Chapters three, nine, eleven, twelve, and thirteen, as well as the sample essays throughout, are maps of previous voyages along this course. Chapter eleven especially, with comments from admissions officers on student essays, will show you routes of clear sailing as well as the dangerous reefs.

2. *Practice.* On your maiden voyage, don't expect to win the America's Cup. You need some practice—the more the better. I have made a few suggestions for ways to strengthen your writing muscles, and even given specific examples. To write well, you have to write. How good you want your college essay to be is up to you.

Throughout the book I concentrate on the writing of a general personal statement, to satisfy one of the Common Application topics. Chapter ten suggests ways to address and streamline the writing of the supplements.

A warning: There's no magic formula for writing the college essay. "Writing," said E. B. White, "is an act of faith, not a trick of grammar." It's not any kind of trick at all, in fact. Your writing is your way of seeing and of thinking, and good college essays have as many guises as the Greek god Proteus, who was always changing shape to slip out of somebody's grasp. You, as a college essayist, must realize how *protean* you can be, too: one minute telling a story, the next confessing and explaining a bias, or reminiscing, or investigating your world like a reporter. All so that you can slip *into* somebody's grasp.

• • •

A word about the examples. Whether a particular essay "worked," no one can say, if by worked we mean it was the crowbar that opened the gate. Some essays, no matter how good, won't get you into First Choice University; some, no matter how bad, won't keep you out (if your parents just paid for the complete renovation of the admissions building, let's say). The essays in this book are naturally taken out of their application contexts, so you don't know who had three A's senior year and who was captain of cross-country. It's not always easy to tell precisely why someone "got in." But a good essay, like a good painting, has an interior rightness that has nothing to do with the price it fetches in the college admissions auction. That rightness makes the difference for you when the decision could go either way. If you write as well as you can, the rest of the process will take care of itself, and you can glide into your senior spring knowing you'll be more than just a list of numbers to the admissions committee.

That's how an essay really *works:* it shows you at your alive and thinking best, a person worth listening to—not just for the ten minutes it takes to read your application, but for the next four years.

GETTING READY

1

THE GRAY AREA

OK, so you're not an A-plus student at HardAss Prep, captain of three sports teams, third author on a published cancer research breakthrough, with 2300 SATs and a grandfather who was seventh president of First Choice University; you're not the caboose in the class either. If you're like most of the hundreds of thousands of applicants to selective colleges every year, you fall into that murky netherworld peopled by those whose credentials are neither easily accepted nor easily denied: the Gray Area.

Don't panic. Everyone's in the Gray Area somewhere. (Almost everyone. If the hot-shot profile above could be you, toss this book like a wedding bouquet back to your classmates in the Gray Area; as long as you don't write an essay about the pleasures of sticking pins into small furry animals, you're First-Choice bound.) In fact, things get a lot grayer if you're not from one of the built-in Lobby Groups in the process: recruited athletes, development prospects (those who can spare a dozen million in pocket change to build the new gym), members of a historically underrepresented group, or children of alumni. All these applicants have special advocates for them in close contact with the admissions committee. Everyone else is Just Folks.

But whether you're Just Folks or belong to a Lobby Group, no one knows or will *ever* know why you, personally and actually, get in or not. Your teachers don't know. The *New York Times* doesn't know. Your parents' neighbor's cousin's sister-in-law who teaches in the med school at First Choice University doesn't know. College Confidential doesn't know. I don't know. (I assure you.) Your college counselors, who may have been admissions officers themselves quite recently before switching over to the side of the angels, don't know.

Yet ignorance, blissful as ever to exercise, maintains its steady stream of theories. Your *this* or *that* was too low (or too high); colleges were looking for one-talent "pointy" (or well-rounded) students; you got a B in physics (didn't take physics), blah blah blah. But the only ones who really know what happens with your application are the small handful of admissions officers who read your file and make the actual decision. That's because the needs of an admissions office, and therefore the "criteria," are always adjusting to shifting ground, such as the number of applicants in any year, the pressure from the basketball team or the math department, the college's history with your high school, and whether the administration is silly enough to take seriously the goofy "rankings" concocted by various media: "The Best 20 Medium-Sized Suburban Colleges for Left-Handed Economics Majors." In the massive Gray Area, the same application that's admitted one year might be rejected the next. There's plenty of luck involved.

Even though quotas are a thing of the past, no college pretends its process is "fair." An example of how it really works is this: "legacies" (children of alumni) are more than twice as likely as Just Folks to be admitted. Another is this: Three fine goalies have been convinced by the hockey coach to apply. The current goalie is a senior. The backup is a junior. The admissions office has "given" the hockey team a certain small number of places in the class. Result: At least one of the goalies applying is going to get in. Period. His grades and test scores may be lower than thousands of Just Folks who've already been rejected, but it doesn't matter. The hockey team needs a goalie.

Of course, plenty of applicants from the Lobbies are in the Gray Area too—those other two goalies, for instance. Still, at a college like Columbia, which in 2011 had just about 35,000 applications for 1,400 places (they admit about 2,400, or just *under* 7 percent, knowing a little over 40 percent will go elsewhere), after the admissions office finishes with the Lobbies there's hardly anything but scraps left for Just Folks. Practically everyone's in the Gray Area at Columbia—as well as at many other colleges with similar selection ratios.

Word of warning and inspiration: Looking down the barrel of stats like these, you have a helpful realization—you can't game the system. I know, I know—then why are you reading this book? Here's why: There's only one route to getting *in*, and that's going *through*—through the self. It's about accepting this rite of passage, with all its tedious elaborations invented for the colleges' own needs, and taking it back from them to use for your own nefarious purposes, *bwoohoohahahaha*.

So all right, I was wrong. You *can* game the system, apparently. A very good book called *The Early Admissions Game* by Christopher Avery, Andrew Fairbanks, and Richard Zeckhauser argues conclusively from an impressive alp of data that Early Decision and Early Action applicants have a measurable advantage. But you already knew that. Still, even that information, now almost ten years old, may be out of date in the fluid admissions world; it might be worse, it might be better. The colleges read that book too. My point is, whether you're applying early or regular, now or later, you can't game the essay.

At best, life in the Gray Area means the admissions committee suspects you're someone who can do the work and even do it well at their school; at worst it means you are indistinguishable from the monsoon of other students with similar backgrounds and credentials who (happily for the colleges) overflow their application pool. This year I heard the director of admissions at an Ivy League college that shall remain nameless (all right, it was Yale) admit that if he flushed the entire admitted class and accepted instead a couple thousand rejects from that year, there would be no appreciable drop in "quality."

So just getting into the Gray Area at First Choice is an accomplishment. Enjoy the Gray Area. (I don't know, imagine you're in Scotland.) The trick, of course, is getting out of the leaden shadow of sameness and into the sunlit tropics of acceptance. To do that, you have to become three-dimensional to the committee. The best way: write a good essay. But first you have to understand the essay in context.

Is it the most important part of the application? No. Don't be under any illusions about that. You can't control whether they want anthropologists or breaststrokers, but if you *are* choo-chooing along contentedly doing the minimum, even the snappiest essay won't deliver you to an Ivy League station.

THE TRANSCRIPT

The honor of "the most important part of your application" belongs to your high school transcript. Admissions officers, in sickness and in health, cherish this document above all others. And the most important part of it is not the grades, it's the courses themselves. Ironically, the transcript—that sterile list—is the one place where your personality is on display most clearly. Admissions officers are looking to see what your interests are and how you challenge yourself in pursuing them given the choices you have.

The highly selective colleges appear, and often are, conservative: They cast a cold eye, rightly or not, on courses they feel are best left to the colleges, like Art History or Psychology. And in some high schools, these courses are in fact 99 percent mental bubblegum. If they are worthwhile at your school, talk to your counselor to make sure the colleges know it.

But most important of all, a highly selective college is interested in students who are interested in the world and in their lives. The best route to a successful application (and beyond, forever!) is to follow your interests in order to discover what you love, and then to pursue it. Haven't found anything to love yet? Congratulations! That's what your education is *for*. Even your required courses are not there to torture you, despite your mud-wrestle with chemistry; requirements let you discover something interesting you might have been too afraid to explore. Requirements are an aid to courage.

But when you do have electives, authentic interest always shows. Some schools, for example, offer independent study programs. Parents and counselors often wring their hands about such a deviation from an imagined Ivy "track" and worry that it looks like fluff on a transcript. But if you're pursuing a passion, you're helping yourself as an applicant. How much? According to calculations, which I am making up as I go along, your application improves exactly 11.3 percent. Seems incredible, doesn't it? Yet that is what the calculations show. If you are taking an independent study course to coast and kick back, that shows, too.

Rigid pronouncements advisers may sometimes make, such as "You must take physics to get into First Choice," are often false, based on rumor, anecdote, and anxiety. If you make your choices on the basis of your real curiosity you will never go wrong.

A note about advanced placement courses: Once a way to earn college credit—few colleges grant it these days—they have now become primarily an admissions tool. An AP class may be a way to indulge your passion for a particular subject. But if you're taking it because you "need to have it on your transcript," then it's not doing you much good and may in fact be hurting you. And all APs are not even created equal. The "same course" varies from school to school, even from teacher to teacher in the same school. Surprise! I know of a school that designates the entire junior year in English as "AP." One suspects (at least, this one suspects, and he is joined by many demanding high schools that have abandoned the AP) that AP courses have become a kind of scam.

Anything you take to "look good" almost infallibly does the opposite.

How do they detect it? Reading 20,000 applications over five months for a few years can go a long way toward teaching the intricacies of teenage (if not human) frailty.

After checking the character of your program, admissions officers naturally look at the grades. (I'm misleading you deliberately here. They don't really look at courses first, grades second; that would be impossible. But I'm giving you an idea of their priorities.) And now for the fifty-thousand-dollar-a-year-tuition question: Is that B in an "honors" or "advanced" course the equivalent of an A in "regular?" If you've been following along, by now you should know the answer: it's the wrong question.

THIS IS ONLY A TEST.
IF IT HAD BEEN A REAL EMERGENCY . . .

Twenty-four years ago I thought the SAT was fading fast as admissions criteria.

Now *there* was a spectacular failure to sniff out the future. Maybe it was just wishful thinking. Certainly I was rosy about the speed of the wane; today any fade in the influence of standardized testing is barely visible to the naked eye.

In fact, there's *more* testing now. Like a gangster coveting rival turf, the ACT—once seen as more of a Midwestern test—has muscled in on the SAT's Eastern and West Coast clientele and now claims to be the most widely accepted entrance test in the country.

But does the SAT sit idly by? No sirree, Bob. First it changes its name, retaining the medieval "Scholastic" and the menacing "Test," but replacing the pretentious and inaccurate "Aptitude" with the safe bureaucracy of "Achievement." That may not seem like a game-changer to you, but in this world of branding, such little shifts apparently matter.

Then the SAT makes another depressingly genius move, in the best-defense-is-a-good-offense category: it adds *another test*, the writing sample, and so another 800 points.

Many students now take both the SAT and the ACT, fishing for the higher score. And so it appears, in our numbers-obsessed dizziness, that standardized testing has (especially at the thirty or so most-selective schools) actually *grown* in importance—although we might also note that when colleges are accepting 10 percent or less of all applicants, *everything* grows in importance.

At the same time, my old (and current) point is that the number of four-year schools that do *not* require *either* the SAT or the ACT is also growing: 815 currently, and the list includes schools such as American University, Bennington, Bard, Bowdoin, Bates, Connecticut College, DePaul, Dickinson, Earlham, Franklin and Marshall, Hampshire, Holy Cross, Lewis and Clark, Mt. Holyoke, Providence College, Sarah Lawrence, University of the South (Sewanee), Smith, and Wake Forest.

Fine schools such as Middlebury, Colby, Hamilton, Colorado College, and Bryn Mawr don't require the 2400–point SATs if a student submits the SAT II subject tests, or the international baccalaureate, or AP scores. The University of Texas at Austin considers the SAT only if its grade-point threshold isn't met.

Whether you should take the SAT or the ACT or both is another one of those questions for which there is no answer. (Statistical folk wisdom says girls and grinds should take the ACT, boys and bright slackers the SAT, but those tendencies, even if real, don't necessarily apply to your particular case. That's one of the problems with statistics. And folk wisdom.)

All this is just to say admissions officers will look on the SAT with a little skepticism *if you give them a reason to.* That means you should come across as you at your most interesting. After all, they've seen too many students with scores way below the class average (admitted for various reasons) wind up four years later in the Cum Laude lists, or become successful alumni who support the college with huge donations.

Admissions officers use the SAT as a reflection of your academic accomplishment versus your background: what have you done with what opportunities you've had? In other words, an 1800 from a Chicago private school boy whose parents, a financier and a lawyer, went to Princeton is not the same as an 1800 from a bilingual Southside public school girl who will be the first in her family to go to college.

In any case, admissions officers know—as even the test makers admit, according to FairTest, the watchdog group that nips insightfully at the heels of all standardized testing—that "people with very different scores on one test administration might get the same scores on a second administration. On the SAT, for example . . . two students' scores must differ by at least 144 points (out of 1600) before they are willing to say the students' measured abilities really differ."

Your statistics-and-probability teacher can tell you something similar: a 600 on one part of the SAT means there's about a 50 percent chance that your score falls between 570 and 630.

What have certainly grown in importance are the SAT IIs, the subject tests, since they seem to admissions people to reflect more of what you're actually learning in school.

Contradictory note about the vast galaxy of test-prep companies spawned by SAT and ACT anxiety: They work, within limits. Evaluate the time such a course demands. I won't say (though I should) that every hour spent on such a course—and they require many hours—is a total waste. I will say that every hour spent on them is one you could have been pursuing your interests, changing the world, discovering the passion of your life—or even just reading a book, fishing, watching a movie with friends, working on your jump shot, making a baguette, playing monsters with your little brother, daydreaming, or any of the other gazillion activities that will make you a far better person than any achievable increase in score points.

Remember that even the transcript and testing together don't tell your whole story to the admissions committee. At Brown, we routinely turned down students with superb grades and high scores. "What does he offer us," we had the luxury of asking, "besides numbers?" The kicker for the committee is still their personal response to you, the flesh on the statistical bones. Where do they find the real you?

THE MYTH OF THE INTERVIEW

Never in the interview. Unlike employers, selective colleges use interviews for public relations, not evaluations. Interviewers are trained (sort of) to be charming and warm, no matter what they think of a candidate. (I know, you had a bland lump of plasma for an interviewer. But just because they are trained doesn't mean they learn; think of your math class.) The object of an interview from the college's point of view is to give you a terrific experience of their school. After all, despite what the interviewer thinks, you may get in. So don't make a stain. You'll be fine.

The interview counts so little because the majority are done by alumni, graduate students, and even undergrads (that's how I got my start in admissions), and admissions officers can't depend on these impressions. They don't even know all their interviewers personally. Another reason is that one shaky conversation in a coffee shop or law office can hardly outweigh four years of your life. The colleges have finally come clean on this. Amherst, for example, says on its application, "we do not offer interviews as part of the application process." Many schools have followed suit. At Tufts and many other colleges, the interview is "optional."

The interview has become one of the most precious recruiting tools a college has, at least partially because it costs them nothing—alumni interviewers volunteer for the job.

TEACHER RECOMMENDATIONS

Still, admissions officers are looking for the real you, not a statistical profile. If not in the interview, then where? One place is certainly in the teacher recommendations, but these are only as good as the teachers writing them. How well does the writer know you and how clearly can he or she paint a portrait of you for a reader? Many recommendations are absolutely crucial in a decision, others much less so.

Here's how to pick a teacher to write for you: Don't automatically go for the one who gave you an A. It should be someone who knows you well and writes well. In an ideal world, you might get to see samples of his or her writing beforehand, but here on earth asking for such a thing might put a wee strain on teacher-student relations. In place of samples you can make an educated guess about a teacher's writing based on his or her teaching. Good teachers are usually good because they communicate vividly, and so are a good bet to write well. Beware the recommendation from the dull, indifferent teacher, even though you aced the difficult course. It will read, "Susan is a very fine student and a nice person who is very thorough and completes all work in a neat and timely manner. She is well groomed, etc."

You don't want *that*. What you need is a letter that will make you come alive—the same specificity and vividness you're searching for in your own essay writing. Once you have such teachers in mind, you naturally want to know whether they'll support you strongly or not. But you can't ask, "Will you write me a good letter for First Choice?" After such a crass question, the chances that it *will* be a good one immediately recede to the vanishing point.

Instead, try, "Would you write my college recommendation?" and then pay close attention. The following answers bode well:

"Sure."

"Happy to."

"Certainly."

And similar responses, given without hesitation. If there is any throat clearing or paper shuffling, find someone else. For instance, a teacher might begin with a slow "Well . . ." or "I'll tell you what—"

"No problem," you say. Then smile and skip out to the hall, where your heart can crash safely into a thousand tiny pieces on the floor. It's hard to take these little rejections, but it's a lot easier than taking a big one from First Choice because of lukewarm recommendations.

If a teacher says, "Have you tried someone else? If you get stuck, come back to me," don't ever come back. Read faces. If the expression says *I have so much work I am in physical pain at the idea of this new burden*, excuse yourself and say, "That's OK, I've got Mr. Schenkler lined up." If you have trouble finding enough people who know you, you've been doing something at school that even the best essay can't repair.

THE MEDIA ARE THE MESSAGE

Some things that aren't part of the application can have a massive, if hidden, effect: Facebook and other social media. It's like Stealth Criteria—you'll never know they saw it. But if you think admissions officers do not check the Facebook pages of applicants, then you're probably not astute enough to be going to college. Put yourself in their shoes—you know you would look. It's too tempting. And remember, with swarms of applicants buzzing in the Gray Area they are only too happy to find reasons to swat some away. So a word to the wise: all those supposedly coded, inside jokes and pictures on your wall about how wasted you got at the Homecoming Party? Uh-uh. Manage your Facebook pages and settings.

RÉSUMÉ

Does an eighteen-year-old really have a résumé? I think not. (OK, if you've been on the Broadway stage since you were nine or have published poems in the *Paris Review*, *Granta*, and *Tin House*, I suppose our judges will allow it.) I know the résumé seems like a concise and time-saving way to answer the questions about activities and extracurricular activities, in the same way that I suggest tailoring one essay to several questions later in this book. But a résumé, especially a professional-looking one, *really* reeks of extreme "packaging," a huge turn-off at the selective schools.

PUBLISH OR PERISH

In the admissions committee's search for who you are, the essay is, in fact, no more important than any other part of the application, with this important difference: it's the only place they can hear *your voice*, just as you want it. One big difficulty with that is obvious: you've probably never written anything like this, and certainly not for an audience you can't (and may never) see. It's not the same as the history paper for Mr. Snoozleman on the causes of the Civil War, or the English assignment for Ms. Hackenbush on the significance of the green light at the end of the dock in *The Great Gatsby*. In those assignments, the readers aren't waiting breathlessly to read your words in order to learn something themselves or take pleasure in what you say; they have probably studied these topics for years. At best such assignments are *exercises*, literary pushups supposedly in preparation for college, but meaningless in themselves. At worst, writing them is not writing at all—you're more like a cat in a lab, coughing up hairballs.

But your college essay is not an exercise; it's a Real Game. It is, in fact, a piece of "published" writing. Like a book or magazine article, it goes out into a world of unknown readers who will judge you without being on your side from the beginning, the way a teacher is. In fact, it disappears into the hellish hole of the admissions office, never to resurface.

Admissions officers are not your friends. (See all those boxes and check-lists on the Common App for your counselor and teacher to check off? The colleges are trying to get your counselor and teacher to do the admissions officer's job, which is to rate the candidates. Those boxes don't help *you*.) Although they are not your friends, admissions officers know more about you, information of a particular kind, than some of your friends do—and most of your teachers as well. At most colleges, the materials in your file are placed in a strict order, beginning with your "numbers": class rank and SATs, which are the first information about you an admissions officer sees on her laptop. You can see from the order of the Common App that by the time admissions officers get to your essay, they know your family and your schoolwork very well. They already know a great deal about your school, and they're seeing certain patterns about you. It's like the moment at the dance: You're standing around the punch bowl when you see *her* arrive. You've seen each other around school, you know each other's names, have a few common friends, and have been in one class together; you've seen her play on the basketball team, and she knows you're the sweeper in soccer. You're acquainted with her, in other words, but you'd like to get to know her much better. OK—now what? What will you do or say that will not be a crock, a tired line, a pathetic pose?

The committee has the same relationship to you: they are acquainted with you, and now you want them to know you better. Understanding all this may seem only to add to your procrastination at first. But you'll be able to use this knowledge to advantage if you approach your college essay the way published writers approach their work:

1. Who is my audience?
2. What kind of piece is it?

3. What do I have to say to these readers? (Not, What do they want to hear?)

Begin at the beginning. Who are these people who hold your fate in their hands? (Actually, they don't hold your fate in their hands—that's your mission, should you choose to accept it. It's far more important who you are and are becoming, now and when you get to college, than which college you go to. You heard it here first.) Now that you know where your essay fits into the application, let's find out where it fits into an admission officer's life.

Breathe and proceed.

2

KNOW YOUR AUDIENCE

At eight P.M. in the bleak heart of winter the bundled figure of a wretched man, perhaps the village bum, drags itself like a troll across the frozen campus of First Choice University in the town of Crewneck, Massachusetts. His hunch and bloodshot eyes of despair speak of sleepless nights, probably on doorstoops and benches. Like a hobo from the 1920s he shuffles and shambles. He makes a pitiful picture.

Yet a closer look under the lowered hat brim reveals an alarmingly young face for one on the fritz. The eyes are full of fatigue, yes, but a peek into his bag reveals no cardboard shoes, half-empty nips, salvaged mosquito netting, nor any of the other sad accessories of street living. Inside the bag, instead, is a laptop computer that will later give him access to a database of 25,000 applicants to First Choice University. This prematurely aged man is twenty-five years old, and he is neither drunk nor destitute (well, one out of two). At this late hour on this bitter night, he is just leaving work. His name is Henry Haggard, and he is an admissions officer in the middle of application-reading season.

Poor Henry is not looking forward to the rest of the evening. While many of his non-admissions friends in Crewneck are already out to dinner and frolic this Thursday night—the beginning of the weekend in all college towns—he still has thirty applications to read by tomorrow. His lone hope for combining business with pleasure is to find others who can share in and sympathize with his drudgery. That leaves only the other members of the admissions staff, with whom he already spends twenty-four hours a day, it seems. But then he thinks of the newest admissions officer, a young woman just graduated from First Choice last spring . . .

Let's fast-forward to later that evening.

SCENE: The living room of Haggard's apartment, decorated with a week's worth of crumpled socks lying across the unmatched secondhand furniture like dead herring. Smashed tortilla chips mingled with rug lint form a crunchy veneer underfoot. In one corner, the television crackles with a basketball game. Henry is stretched out on the couch, propped half-awake with a few pillows on one end, shifting restlessly under his laptop. Now and then he rouses himself to type, trancelike, for a few minutes and subsides again into the pillows. He has spent most of his evenings this month—in fact the last four winters of his life—in this position. In his imagination tonight the inside of his refrigerator looms in Technicolor, the frosted green glass of the beer bottles beckoning to him like beautiful mermaids across an endless murky gulf of application forms.

On the other side of the room, sunk in a low-slung armchair, is Sarah Bleary—twenty-one, bright, vivacious, but already sprouting dark circles under the eyes in this, her first admissions season. Laptop on her knees, she stares numbly at the screen. The two of them push at the keys like drugged seals. Their eyes are glassy from long hours of close work.

BLEARY: You sure know how to show a girl a good time.

HAGGARD: Welcome to life in the fast lane.

BLEARY: Hey, here's an essay for you. *(He does not look up. She reads from the application.)* "I believe breadth of learning is the most important educational goal to have—"

HAGGARD *(Putting his hands over his ears)*: No more, I can't take it. Not while the Celtics are down ten points.

BLEARY *(Going on)*: "For me breadth has a double advantage: Firstly, it is to anyone's advantage to know about as much as they can, and secondly, there are more than one or two things in which I am interested. I am not saying that it is not good to concentrate studies in one area later on, or that I want to learn all there is to learn, but rather that my four college years will be my chance to take a wider range of courses than I ever could, and I intend to take this opportunity." No E. B. White, is he?

HAGGARD: The imagination of a hockey puck.

BLEARY: I've been reading ones like these all night. But the thing is, he's a decent kid—I want to like him.

HAGGARD: There's your first mistake.

BLEARY *(Intent on the application)*: He's got OK grades in a good courseload at a good school, he's on the tennis team and volunteers at the hospital, but just so gray on paper. He wouldn't stand out against a cement wall.

HAGGARD: Here's your write-up. *(Eyes closed, dictating)* "Respectable stats and the usual range of x-currics but bland bland bland. Teachers mention imagination and sense of humor not confirmed by essay. A numbers call at the end, but looks like WL at best."

BLEARY: How can you say that without even reading the file? Besides, you're wrong about the imagination and humor. They say he's earnest and hardworking.

HAGGARD: So change it to, "Implied drudgery is indeed confirmed by essay." I know that kid and thousands like him. Standard fare from private schools in Boston or New York or Chicago—

BLEARY: It's Dallas, actually.

HAGGARD: Same difference. Probably has New York parents.

BLEARY *(Confirming it in the file)*: All right, smart guy—

HAGGARD: Or maybe he's from high-tax-bracket public schools in the middle-class 'burbs. Big difference, right? What's so likable?

BLEARY: A little cynical, aren't we?

HAGGARD: Just realistic. Wait'll you've been at it a couple of years. Or months. *The kids gotta come across on paper,* or else when they come up for committee decision you—and they—won't have a leg to stand on. I mean, I like to discover an NSTK as much as anyone—

BLEARY: NSTK?

HAGGARD: Neat Small Town Kid. But even they gotta come alive in the app. Haven't you noticed that most apps are the same as most others? These are teenagers, after all. I know they've really worked hard as assistant business manager of the newspaper and they're all individuals and "very unique" and all of that crap—at least, that's what they all say—but you wouldn't know it from their applications. And that's what counts. I've got no patience for the No-Pulse Brigade.

BLEARY *(Yawning)*: What time is it?

HAGGARD *(Cheering up)*: Beer time.

BLEARY *(Pats her laptop)*: Duty still beckons.

HAGGARD: Duty doesn't have to be *total* agony.

BLEARY: Yeah, well. I've been on this same kid for half an hour and I can't remember a thing about him. I think I'll get some more coffee.

HAGGARD: Why don't you cut out the middle man and go straight to the No-Doz? There's not enough coffee in Brazil to keep you alert for forty files. Have a beer—might as well enjoy yourself.

BLEARY: Don't try to corrupt me—I'm on a strict caffeine and popcorn diet. Besides, I'll fall asleep.

HAGGARD: That never stopped anyone from reading files. Sure, you'll have the occasional nightmare that every kid is a pre-something-or-other whose essay begins, "Hello, I am a very unique person," but you'll get over it. Some of my best evaluations were written asleep. It's like the Ouija board. The pencil moves by itself. *(He struggles up from the couch and goes into the kitchen.)*

BLEARY: How do people do this job for ten or fifteen years?

HAGGARD *(From the kitchen)*: Don't ask me.

BLEARY: Didn't I hear this was your last year?

HAGGARD: Yup. My hitch for Mother First Choice is over. *(Returning with coffeepot and two beer bottles)* Law school, here I come.

BLEARY: It's not over yet.

HAGGARD: True. *(He holds out a bottle.)* Brought one for you just in case. Sure you don't want some? *(She shakes her head. He pours from the coffeepot into her cup.)*

BLEARY: Maybe a sip of yours. *(He hands her the beer; she sips and gives it back.)* Mmmm.

HAGGARD *(Prone again)*: I'll tell you how they do it. The big wheels don't read as many files, for one thing.

BLEARY: Assistant directors do.

HAGGARD *(Sitting up halfway)*: Hey, *I'm* an assistant director. Assistant director means squat. You'll be assistant director too if you stay around two, three years and don't have any major screw-ups. I mean the directors and associate directors, the honchos. You think they read half the files you do? No way. Too much burnout.

BLEARY: What I can't believe is the amount of paperwork, all the computer junk. I guess I thought of it as mostly meeting kids and parents, choosing the class, that kind of thing. There're plenty of good parts, like all the expense-account travel—

HAGGARD: Join the admissions office and see Tulsa.

BLEARY *(Ignoring him)*:—and the long vacation, and the people. It's a great job for someone just out of school. But there's a lot of diddly detail, too. I mean, we're talking petty bureaucracy here.

HAGGARD: You got it. Today was typical. I spent most of the morning emailing alumni and guidance counselors, doing my blog for the office, emailing a follow-up to a great kid I saw in Colorado, and reading precisely three files. In the afternoon I had to finish filling out my travel vouchers and writing the reports on my last trip, had a meeting with the Diversity Office on recruiting in the southwest, and then we had that full staff meeting at the end. Total file reading: six. Thirty-four to go—not counting the ones I had left over from yesterday and the day before that.

BLEARY: You're behind?

HAGGARD: You're kidding, right?

BLEARY: I thought I was the only one.

HAGGARD: Everybody is. I wouldn't worry about it too much. Everything is designed to get in the way of file reading.

BLEARY: Including bull sessions?

HAGGARD: Hey, even oxen get to take the yoke off once in a while. How far behind are you?

BLEARY: Far.

HAGGARD: How long does it take you to do a file?

BLEARY: I don't know, fifteen minutes or so, with writing it up and everything. I guess longer when I get tired.

HAGGARD: Well, there it is. Not bad, but you've gotta do five or six an hour to keep from drowning. Ten minutes and get outta there. And hell, even that doesn't do it. What you realize is that, to do the job right, there aren't enough hours. And that is why God invented winter weekends.

BLEARY: Ten minutes? How do you give it a good read?

HAGGARD: After a while, most of them won't even take five. The point is to get them done. Period. Sure you'll blow a couple; that's expected. But there are checks and balances along the way in the system. Even so, occasionally a kid falls through the cracks. Can't be helped. Things happen fast. They have to.

BLEARY: I *was* a little blown away by the speed of the early-action decisions in committee. I mean, boom boom boom, most kids took no more than two minutes.

HAGGARD *(Shakes his head)*: Oh boy. Wait'll regular committee starts in February. Two minutes is an eternity. The December meetings are like stop-action slow motion compared to March. Last year we made four hundred forty-four decisions in *one day* between ten o'clock and four—and we broke for lunch for half an hour! Of course, those were New Jersey applicants, so it doesn't really count.

BLEARY *(laughing)*: Careful, I'm from Teaneck.

HAGGARD: I knew there was something weird about you. But we see so many apps from there that we go to committee with them specially prepped for speed. We took—what?—ten percent overall last year; you know what the New Jersey percentage was?

BLEARY: Something like eight, no?

HAGGARD: Five. Five percent! Jersey alums went postal over that. But listen, that's true—about the lower ratio, I mean—in every area where we get a ton of apps.

BLEARY: It won't be much better this year if the kids I'm seeing are any indication. I don't know why, but the last few days have been full of essays on dying pets by the pom-pom crowd. And I've still got a bunch to go. Speaking of which . . .

HAGGARD: Yeah, yeah. *(They return to their screens, occasionally shaking their heads or laughing over an application. Sarah sips at her coffee, henry quaffs the beer. He starts on the second bottle.)*

BLEARY: Listen to this one.

HAGGARD: I warn you, what you're about to do constitutes assault with a deadly weapon in some states.

BLEARY *(Reading from the essay)*: "I, Bradley T. Borewell, am a happy, well-rounded student. Through hard work and much study I have been able to produce this result."

HAGGARD *(Sighting down the barrel of an imaginary rifle)*: Bang. It was self-defense, Your Honor.

BLEARY *(Yawning and stretching)*: I think today's exercise in sadomasochism is over.

HAGGARD: Going so soon?

BLEARY *(Getting up and looking at the kitchen clock)*: It's almost midnight. There're still some left, but as you would say, what's tomorrow for, right? *(She goes to the closet for her coat and packs her laptop into its case.)*

HAGGARD: If it weren't so late that it will be early soon, I might ask what you're doing later. I might ask you anyway.

BLEARY: Very amusing, Henry.

HAGGARD: Admissions officers are people too, you know.

BLEARY: Doesn't feel like it. I feel like a file-reading marionette. Wind me up and I do forty a day.

HAGGARD: If you're lucky.

BLEARY: See you tomorrow. Thanks for the coffee. And the wild times. *(She moves toward the door. Still on the couch, he twists and stretches out his arms in mock panic.)*

HAGGARD: No no, don't leave me here alone with *them!* *(But she is gone. Henry slumps back and looks at his screen.)*

HAGGARD: Five more. But first . . .

(He goes into the kitchen and returns with another beer. Settling on the couch, his eyes half-lidded, he gets back to his computer, and hits return to open up his next file, his thirty-eighth of the day—YOUR APPLICATION.)

Fadeout, with the sound of snoring and the distant roar of the televised crowd.

WHAT IT MEANS

This is your audience. Study them well. Not exactly the Nobel Prize panel. There are other members of the committee, of course, each of them different, but Henry and Sarah are common types. There are actually two basic species of admissions officer—the Temps *(Miserabilis overworkus)* and the Lifers *(Cynica terminus)*. The Temps are likely to be young, enthusiastic, and often recently graduated from the school they're working for. They're intelligent but not usually bookish, and hired largely for their sales appeal; the wholesome extrovert abounds among young admissions officers.

Temps are interested in using admissions work as an interesting time-killer until they enter graduate school or business or, now and then, college academics. Some end up in high schools as teachers and guidance counselors. Henry Haggard and Sarah Bleary are Temps.

Lifers, on the other hand, at the top level, are the big guns who set policy and run the show. Just below that is a class of itinerant admissions soldiers, Lifers all, who move from school to school, slowly climbing the ladder toward a directorship somewhere. Many of them began, in their salad days, as Temps, but got caught up in the business through inclination or inertia. Few prepare to be Lifers—it just happens. Some are hardcore bureaucrats, and some have fallen into a comfortable career from more precarious faculty jobs. (Tenured professorships—the only secure college teaching appointments—are difficult to get.) Admissions offers lots of benefits—reasonable job security, free tuition for family members, good vacations, and in most cases a lovely and lively place to live.

Lifers these days are usually personally dynamic, multitasking market-savvy "enrollment managers" who see the job as stewardship of the "brand." They don't read as many files as Temps, though they do wield more weight in policy, and many are remarkably familiar with the details of the class.

(This seems as good a place as any to mention the obvious: Incompetence occurs as frequently in admissions offices as it does elsewhere, which is to say, with discouraging semiregularity. There's not much you can do about this, but it might soften the blow if you're rejected. "They wouldn't know something good if it hit them in the face," you can say. But, like umpires who may now and then blow a call, admissions offices are not known for changing their decisions.)

Both Temps and Lifers are great at parties. They are outgoing and charming, professional interviewers and minglers and smilers. Somewhere underneath it all, in most cases, is legitimate interest in education or in kids, but between the superficial smiles and the deeper sympathy grows a very stubborn layer of um, *experience*. (I'm trying not to say cynicism.) It blisters rapidly into callus, even in the newest recruits. These are your readers.

WHO DECIDES?

The Temps and the early Lifers do the bulk of the application reading. In fact, most admissions offices hire outside readers, from graduate students to deans' spouses, to pick up the slack. The more seniority you have, the fewer files you read. It's understandable. File reading is the drudge work, and directors want to look at the big picture. The irony is that the readers have less to say about policy but more about individual decisions—more therefore about your application, especially if you're in the Gray Area.

FIRST AND SECOND READING

Most files are read twice. Henry and Sarah are in stage one. Theirs are the first comments to darken your file. (They also rate you *numerically* as a student and as a person, usually on a scale from one to five or six.) Colleges handle first reading differently. At Brown, we always first-read applications at random; only later does the admissions officer covering your geographical area, the person who is going to present you to the committee—and essentially make the decision on you—read your application. At Columbia, on the other hand, files were first-read by the officer in charge of your area and second-read randomly by faculty, grad students, and anyone else the admissions office can corral to help ease the load.

At some colleges, though, every file doesn't even get to the director. Applicants are screened by a few readers in a "regional committee." Admissions officers will tell you that only the obvious rejects don't make that first cut, but built into such a system is great pressure to trim the workload of the director's final committee and to *save time*. You can bet that almost everyone who's weeded out early belongs to Just Folks.

Some math: If a school has 30,000 applicants, even if the committee meets every single day between November 1 and April 1, including Thanksgiving, Christmas, and New Year's—which of course it doesn't— the college is making 200 decisions a day, or 25 per hour. That's less than two minutes per file. But if, as is true, the committee meets about a hundred days, they're doing 300 a day, or almost 40 an hour if they push hard. That's why many colleges have more than one committee, which means the director may *never* see your application.

At all the colleges, it is the reading of the *area person* that counts most—the second reader in a process like Brown's, the first in one like Columbia's. The area officer looks at you in relation to other applicants from your school and your region. The area person literally "knows where you're coming from."

RIFFRAFF READERS
Faculty

You are not writing for a panel of professors. Although at smaller colleges a faculty member or two may be more involved in admissions—they may even be given time off to work in the office—decisions are made overwhelmingly by Temps and Lifers. Admissions officers wish it were not so, but faculty at schools like the Ivy colleges are not typically concerned with the admissions operation, except to howl occasionally that the freshmen in their classes can't write English. The last thing professors want to do is read twenty files a day.

Hired Guns

Many colleges employ part-time readers to trim the application population. These may include anyone from graduate students to the dean's relatives by marriage. Hired-gun readings are often wild cards. They do not share the embattled admissions office psyche, and so they sometimes read the files more carefully (because they read only a few). They have quirkier tastes. But the subtleties of grades and schools are a code they only dimly understand; the hired gun therefore almost always leans heavily on the essay, a document everyone understands, and which speaks (you hope) plainly in your favor.

THE COMMITTEE MEETING

By the time your application gets to the "full" admissions committee—usually the director, the presenter, and one or two other officers (everybody else is busy reading files)—the decision is made. Very rarely does the committee overturn the presenter's recommendations, and such reversals often involve an applicant from one of the Lobby groups. In fact, in the case of an experienced Temp who has established credibility, the committee is likely to be just a rubber stamp.

SCENE: A richly appointed old room in the admissions building at First Choice, with dark wood paneling, a wood and marble fireplace, and recessed mahogany bookshelves. On the walls are original prints of First Choice as it looked in colonial times. In the center of the room, in high-backed chairs around a massive antique oval table polished to a high gloss, sit Henry Haggard, today's presenter; at his left, the director; and across from Haggard, Sarah Bleary—the "committee." The table is besieged

with coffee cups, water bottles, a pizza box, a few clementines, two bananas, a bag
of vanilla-covered pretzels, two bowls of carrot sticks with dip, a half-eaten red vel-
vet cake, some assorted boxes of cookies, and several soda cans. In front of each of
the participants is an open laptop that shows a summary of each application—the
SAT's, class rank or GPA, and various formulas made of that information, as well as
the all-important ratings (1 to 6 at First Choice) already given each file by two admis-
sions readers. The entire application, including the essay, is also available for view
and discussion.

DIRECTOR: What've you got?

HAGGARD: Seven Admits, ninety-seven Rejects, ten Wait List. And a great
YouTube for happy hour.

DIRECTOR: You're tough.

HAGGARD: We're talking about the Bronx, here.

DIRECTOR: OK. Shoot.

HAGGARD: Bronx Polytech first. Black girl with good numbers, no dad, oldest
of four, all brothers, mom's a nurse, easy A. *(As he will do for every decision, the*
director types the proper code. He looks up.) Another easy one, astro numbers but
not a nerd, works part-time with the homeless, teachers ecstatic, two varsity
sports—nothing special, but still—and a great essay about his best friend—

DIRECTOR: OK.

HAGGARD: Next one's not so easy, but a good one, I think. Some spark here.

DIRECTOR: Readers are high for a kid with those numbers.

HAGGARD: Super recs, grades are solid in a strong program, and check out the
essay. "I do some of my best thinking in the bathroom," it starts. [See p. 141.]

DIRECTOR *(Glancing at it)*: C'mon.

HAGGARD: Yup. But he plays it out really well—funny, thoughtful, really sharp. You don't see many like this. Here's the kid you want in your class.

DIRECTOR: If he doesn't spend all his time in the john. *(Director types the admit code.)* Who's next?

HAGGARD: Next one I wanted you to see before we hang him out to dry.

DIRECTOR: Wait list? Those stats are awfully good compared to the Bathroom Buddha.

HAGGARD: Pre-med and flat as a pancake personally. Unbelievably dumb essay, school just repeats the obvious about math-science ability, and teachers are polite. Has a two-page *résumé*.

DIRECTOR: God.

BLEARY: This the kid I read?

HAGGARD: Yup.

BLEARY: The essay's all about how working with microbes made him a better person. He's deadly.

HAGGARD: His dad's some kind of research doctor, that's how he got the lab job.

DIRECTOR: Why not an R? What's keeping him in? You're saying he doesn't offer us a thing.

HAGGARD: I'd be for an R but the school would go nuts. Because that's all we're—

DIRECTOR *(Scrolling down)*: That's it at old Bronx Poly? Nineteen rejects?

HAGGARD: That's right.

DIRECTOR *(Entering the code)*: I don't want to hear from them on this.

HAGGARD: I'll take care of it. They've got a pretty good idea what's coming. It was a weak class.

DIRECTOR: Next.

HAGGARD: Minuet High . . .

Get the idea? The director doesn't even have *time* to read the essay. He sees the beginning, perhaps, and skims the rest. The director wants to spend the minimum amount of time on a case, so the other admissions officers read the essay *for* him, in effect. The readers, and especially the area person, make the difference.

Let's look in some detail at the ways applicants unwittingly make all this speed possible.

3

DANGER: SLEEPY PROSE AHEAD

(or, The Sandman Cometh)

Now you've gotten a glimpse of the road your application will travel and had a peek at your reading audience. You've seen the piles of folders that fill up their houses and their lives like big clumps of fallen leaves over a sewer, a blockage that naturally begins to affect the flow of minor details like eating and sleeping. You know that when they're poring bug-eyed over twenty or thirty or forty applications a day, they're liable to let sleeping essays lie. And *your* application may be in that stack—it may be number thirty-eight. Your first job, then, is this: prevent them from falling asleep.

Go back to the writer's questions: What kind of piece is it? The word *essay* comes from the French word that means "attempt." It's a short piece not intended to exhaust the subject—or the reader. Even among essays, the college essay is a form all its own, with conventions and clichés that admissions officers like Henry Haggard, lying catatonic at midnight on couches all across the country, know only too well. You, as a practitioner of the form, should know them too, and steer clear. (Admissions officers may be tired, but it's hardly your responsibility to *help* them catch up on sleep.) Let's hack into Henry Haggard's database for some of the most common snooze potions whipped up by seniors. We don't have to dig very deep:

1. The Trip. This is the one about the visit to Europe, Israel, Kansas, or other exotic land. Applicants make The Trip in the company of family, peers, or even alone in one of the many programs that take students into the home of a foreign family to live. But wherever they are, 99 percent of the travelers seem determined to ignore the small and homely (but significant) details around them in favor of sweeping banalities: "I had to adjust to a whole new way of life. The first thing I noticed was the food, which was very different, as were all the customs; my adopted family's habits were quite different from anything I was used to, but, by the end of my stay, I had come to accept them. I realized that neither I nor they were wrong, but simply different." These essays, as you may be able to guess by now, are *not* very different. It seems that all writers of The Trip "eventually got used to all the cultural differences" and "finally felt like part of the family." But where are the colors and textures and flavors of something seen and experienced fresh?

These travels, of course, "broadened my horizons" and "gave me a new perspective on my native land, the United States." Often, applicants report that living in a foreign country, whose language they had been studying in school, "increased my fluency and facility immensely." Surprise!

Also well trampled are the Trip paths leading to vague forms of self-discovery in far-flung ancestral homelands. "I got a very religious feeling from the Sistine Chapel and I was proud to be an Italian." These essays usually show the strong influence of the brochures and airplane travel magazines from which they were lifted. At the end of the Ancestral Trip, writers swell with pride and platitudes at having "learned more than I ever could in history class about my cultural heritage."

Even wilderness trips, like Outward Bound, can somehow get boiled down into this soggy formula. "On my trip to the Grand Tetons, I learned to work with people and stretch my abilities to the utmost." Change the first phrase to "In my work as a terrorist," and the sentiment still holds.

2. My Favorite Things. This "list" essay (save your lists for your poems) is usually written in a hand which dots its *i*'s with little circles and often takes off from an opening something like, "Things I am for: puppy dogs, freedom, big soft pillows, and Mrs. Field's cookies. Things I am against: nuclear war, pimples, racial discrimination, spinach." Written by males and females alike, it is the unmistakable sign of what we used to call the Fluffball.

3. Miss America. The Big Issue questions, like "Please comment on an issue of national or international concern," lead a lot of people into this trap. "I think World Peace is the most important issue facing us today . . ." and so on like a beauty queen. Equally flimsy stuff pops up about almost any front-page issue—the economy, global warming, the Middle East.

At best these pieces sound like the small-town editorials of outraged old ladies. The arguments, no matter how powerfully right you feel, no matter how seriously you study the topic in school or debate it across the dinner table, are plagiaristic and generic. Admissions committees do not want to know how slavishly you can regurgitate views of parents, teachers, or cable news networks.

4. Jock. This is not a topic as much as a whole way of thinking, so it is certainly not confined to essays by neckless mouth-breathers. It seems to have spread like mildew into writing on every activity students pursue and is by far the most common approach among earnest and intelligent students trying too hard to impress an admissions committee. Musicians, actors, lab interns, yearbook editors, club officers—students from every walk of high school life have succumbed to the questionable charms of the Jock essay, flocking like doomed ducks to a wooden decoy. Still, though, scholar-athletes sound its most familiar and resonant note: "Through wrestling I have learned to set goals, to go all out, and to work with people." Now *that's* a frightening prospect.

Anyone can (and too many do) fill in this formula: Through *blank*

(piano playing, spider collecting, candle-pin bowling) I have learned
Noble Value A, High Platitude B, and Great Lesson C. The result affects
an admissions officer like sodium pentathol and doesn't show anything
about you, except that you may have succeeded in spending seventeen
happy, thought-free years.

5. My Room. A common variation on number two. "I don't know what
to tell you about myself, so I guess I'll describe my room. That just about
says it all." This opening is followed by a highlighted tour up and down
the room's Himalayas of DVDs, devices, baseball gloves, and miscella-
neous junk, accompanied by some self-conscious (and very old) jokes
about messes and cleanliness: "Anyway, a clean desk is the sign of an
empty mind." So is this essay.

6. Three D's. Another recipe that tries to tell readers what to think of
you. "I honestly believe that I have the *d*iscipline and *d*etermination and
*d*iversity of interests to succeed at whatever I do." Maybe. But probably
not at the college that receives an essay beginning with that line, because
those three D's equal one more: *dull*.

7. Tales of My Success (or, The Time I Won My Town the Race). A particularly deadly Jock/Three D combination. "But, finally, when I crossed
the finish line first and received the congratulations of my teammates,
I realized all the hard work had been worth it." Why must all stories of
sports, elections, and other "challenges" (there's another cliché for you)
end on a note of Napoleonic triumph? Or, if not triumph, then the righ-
teous tone of the principled crusader who stood for what was right but,
alas, went down to defeat. Other people will be more persuasive about
your success—teachers, counselors.

8. Pet Death. Maudlin descriptions of animal demise, always written
by the Fluffball. "As I watched Buttons's life ebb away, I came to value the
important things in this world."

9. The Perspirant. Writing about "a challenge you've faced," students sometimes allow their anxiety to lead them into "This essay is the greatest challenge I have ever faced. . . ." The other Common App topics may tempt you to write about the process of applying. Listen carefully here: DO NOT WRITE ABOUT THE PROCESS OF APPLYING! We used to describe such applicants as "sweaty." If you don't have anything more worthwhile to write about than the application itself, it leads a reader to the inescapable idea you don't have much to add to campus life.

10. Selling and Telling—Autobiography. Trying to say anything meaningful about a whole life in five hundred words can reduce any writer to absurdity. So if your essay begins, "Hello, my name is . . ." your application is going into the cyber hole from which nothing escapes. If you've gotten anything out of this book so far, you probably won't make such a simple gaffe, though every year a surprising number of perfectly capable students do.

Other autobiographical strategies are only slightly better. "I am a very unique person with many interests and abilities and goals." Would *you* want to read three hundred of those?

The Family Salute is another. "I come from a close-knit family. I have a very close relationship with my parents and siblings"—not sisters and brothers, notice—"and my eighty-three-year-old grandmother and I are especially close." The writer's parents may have been close for years (once, at least, they were *very* close) and are probably standing close behind her as she writes her essay. But admissions officers do not get close to the writer, her eyes and ears and mind and heart.

One more word about the pitfalls of the autobiography. I knew an admissions officer who used to pick up his pencil when he noticed too many sentences beginning with a capital *I*. Then he'd start circling them. When the total number of circles got too high for him to bear, he simply recommended a reject and went on to the next file.

• • •

Henry Haggards nationwide are snoring like polar bears over these essays because students writing them are still asking, "What do they want on those college essays?" The point is, you can't force the committee into liking you. You can't tell them what to think. Admissions officers are unusually well equipped with a device Ernest Hemingway prescribed for writers: "a built-in shock-proof shit detector." They're awfully hard to snow with strategies of any kind—no one hates the hard sell more than an admissions officer.

By now, you may be thinking I've blown all your ideas out of the water. Hang on. There are ways to get them to like you without a lot of advertising talk and salesmanship, without assigning yourself a sampling of virtues you think sound good, without empty take-no-chances rhetoric. In fact, getting rid of all those things improves your prospects immediately.

How do you do it? What's left to write about?

Everything.

WRITING

4

CHILLING OUT
(or, Everything I Say You Can't Do, You Can Do)

Consider the following opening of an essay, a blast from the past that might seem dated—but its value as an example is immortal. It seems at first to be a typical "Hello" autobiography.

> I was born on October 22, 1960. There is nothing remarkable about this except that I spent the Sixties in a state of semiconsciousness and missed out on the Beatles. These days, though, a beginning like that seems somehow depressing, and I am not consoled by the fact that there were probably millions of others who had the misfortune to be born at the tail end of the baby boom. I don't think I can ever forgive my parents for not acting sooner.

There is authority and humor here, and awareness. He realizes that his opening is ordinary, and he plays on it surprisingly in the second line by showing that he knows it's banal; at the same time he begins to see some meaning in something as simple as his birthdate. We realize, in fact, that he was setting us up with that first line. We're having fun, suddenly. It's as if we are hiking through a wilderness with an expert outdoorsman; none of us is quite sure where the next step will be, but we have confidence the journey will be worthwhile. The sound is fresh. The turns of thought are surprising. We are hearing a *voice*. The joke at the end brings more than a smile—it steers a reader to the point of the essay: why being born in 1960 was such a big deal. Let's listen to the answer.

Most of my generation (at least this is what *US News and World Report* tells me) lament that by the time we became pubescent we were merely stranded in the wake of something big that had happened. None of us, certainly not I, knew at first what we had missed, but the realization that our generation would be only a few lines in *The American Pageant* while our older brothers and sisters would be appended and multi-footnoted hit me like the first blast of winter. It seemed, when this moment of consciousness came, that there was nothing left to do in a worn-out world. Everything that should have been done or tried had been done or tried. A large portion of it had failed, which only decreased the probability that it would be attempted again in my time. All that the *real* children of the Sixties could do was play records made by people and organizations no longer in the papers. When my world view came of its own (that is, when I was allowed to cross a two-way street by myself) I saw behind me a decade that couldn't be matched and ahead of me a generation that wasn't about to try. Knowing that my life was effectively doomed to dullness somewhat lessened the impact of the axiom that each day should be a new learning experience. What was so new? All I had to do to find out anything important was ask a twenty-one-year-old or read old copies of *Life*. I could, of course, wait for the next revolution. Ideally, I could start another, but the disease which I so readily diagnosed in others applied to me just as well. I didn't really care; it was much easier to fantasize. The idea that the Sagging Seventies were made to be played out with every part prewritten in the style of *As The World Turns*, with neither interest nor importance of action, had solidified in my mind, and in the words of Arlo Guthrie, "There was a-nothing I could do about it."

But also I knew there must be something more than the fact of late arrival, something within my peers and me which put us in our state. As I look around at the classes of '78, I can see little or nothing of passionate commitment. I perceive no idealism, no hate, no guilt, and no audacity. All I can see is thousands of would-be doctors and lawyers who want nothing more than to live in Garden City. For me, their goal leads to erosion of the soul and higher property taxes. I mean, I know I'm seventeen and think that I'm going to live forever and I really should plan for the year 1989, but the idea that my generation will become the Era of Public Accountancy is frightening. I don't want my friends to clean up after the last mess; I want us to make our own.

In my analysis of what everything would be like should the UN suddenly decide to make me king of the world, I don't want riots in the streets or pillaging. I want intelligence of purpose rather than a prefabricated existence. The Seventies are not over yet, and where people are concerned—even where I am concerned—there is always hope. Wherever I go to college, I want least of all to see and be part of the continuation of the Null Generation. I want us to be just as much a part of history as our older brothers and sisters.

Maybe finishing out the decade won't be so bad after all. I mean, I can always go to see *Beatlemania*.

NO BAD TOPICS

But, you say, that essay falls right into the forbidden modes—it could be either the Autobiography or the Big Issue. Relax. Contradiction Number

One: Everything I say you can't do, you can do. There are no good or bad topics for college essays, only good or bad essays. John Updike said, "There is a great deal to be said about almost anything. Everything can be as interesting as every other thing." Sometimes good writing is just the result of reinvigorating what has become a cliché. In your essay, you don't have to say something startling and new, or strain to be "different." The writer above doesn't make any contributions to the store of human knowledge. He just says what he knows in a fresh way that allows us to *see for ourselves* who he is.

This doesn't diminish the danger in all the deadly essays in chapter three, but now that you know the traps of the Terrible Ten, you are ready to understand that most of them—Big Issue, Trip, Autobiography, even Pet Death—can be lively and revealing. Even the old second-grade standby, My Summer Vacation, can lead to excellent writing (see chapter twelve, "Summer Beyond Wish").

You can make a college essay out of *anything;* the materials are everywhere. You just have to pay attention and teach yourself to care.

GETTING READY TO WRITE

Approach is everything. Here are some ideas to keep in mind as you begin.

1. If you ask what "they" are looking for, you are already on the wrong track. What do *you* have to say? That's what they want to hear. The Common App topics are all reducible to "anything you want." Take them at their word. If the thing that intrigues you most lately is that your seven-year-old sister is the one person in the house who can text with one hand without looking, write about that, not World Peace; you have the beginnings of a good Big Issue essay.

2. Find a reader, or readers. Friends, brothers or sisters, pen pals, maybe a teacher you know and trust; *someone* who will respond to your writing in the right spirit. I can't emphasize this enough. You are writing for readers now, and you need to train yourself to say something worth reading. They should simply be people who like good writing and can read your work without preconceived notions about what it should say. They have to be honest, and they have to care about you. It is often mutually inspiring to have your reader(s) also applying to college. You can swap ideas and frustrations. One warning about parents, though. They may want you to "sell yourself," an approach that is dead wrong.

Parents have their uses, but reading your college essay isn't usually one of them. They care too much, and often don't know quite enough, or they have suspect sources of information and want to "fix" everything.

3. Write something only you could write. It should have a sound as distinctive as your speaking voice. The problem with most essays is that they could have been written by anyone. In one sense, your writing "voice" is simply a polished version of your speech; but remember how that speech changes when you're talking to different audiences, like teachers or friends. It's the same you, but your word choice, tone, sentence rhythms, and even the sound of your voice change. Just as you speak in a different "voice" to parents and friends, so you must find the one that's right for this purpose. The voice you should be aiming at is one you'd use toward an acquaintance you wanted to be better friends with. (Remember, admissions officers already know you when they read your essay.) Though it's not the voice you'd use with your *best* friend, it's not formal, either. Don't write to impress an adult, in what you imagine is an "educated" voice. You have two or three different voices of your own, and you should explore and use them. A good essay is like an interesting letter from someone you once met.

4. *Know what you write about*. This is a slight twist on the common writing advice, "Write about what you know." The professional writers in chapter twelve know a lot—everything from history and foreign languages to the design of playing cards. That's part of the reason their writing is good. But be comforted. Writing is discovery—writers often don't realize what they know about something until they try to discuss it in print. If you find you don't know anything well enough to write about it thoughtfully or entertainingly, you've learned something disturbing but not irreversible. And you're wrong—you know more than enough. Think of yourself as a reporter working on a story, the subject of which happens to be your own life and interests. Your memory is your file drawer, and in that file are your research materials. You're looking for *significant details*. These appear in the humblest and most ordinary things you do every day, usually in a more interesting way than they do in the Big Moments (being elected student body president, or scoring the winning water polo goal), events in which so many college essayists try unsuccessfully to Find Meaning. Instead, how about paying attention to that pigeon on your windowsill and what you eat for lunch—and why. If the unexamined life is not worth living, it's certainly not worth writing about.

5. *A college essay is an informal, or familiar, piece*. All the questions, even the Big Issues, are really asking for some kind of personal statement. Don't even think of it as school-related writing. It is not a history or English paper. Loosen up. You are after the most natural tone and style possible—a kind of inspired conversation, scrubbed clean of all its hesitations, repetitions, and vagueness. It is as personal as a phone call.

6. *Entertain*. I don't mean you have to do stand-up where laughs must arrive every fifteen seconds. But all writing entertains at some level. "Entertainment" has gotten a bad name over the years, a reputation as a lightweight; people say, "It isn't a very thought-provoking movie; it's pure entertainment." As if only things that turn your mind into fruit punch are entertaining! To truly entertain doesn't mean to open with a few lame jokes or to sink everything to the level of TV sitcom; it means to sustain a voice worth listening to. You can be as serious or as frivolous as you like, whatever suits you. But when you write, write to give pleasure to your audience. You'll write a more impressive essay than if you set out only to impress.

A WORD ABOUT HUMOR

You'll hear a great deal of conflicting advice about humor. Counselors, teachers, and parents often talk about humor as if it should (and could) be confined like a noisy chicken, occasionally let out for a good squawking and then locked up again in its dingy coop while we get on with really important business. "Oh, humor has its place," they may say, "but not in your college essay." "You can't be sure admissions officers share your idea of what's funny."

Wrong.

Nothing very good was ever written by someone afraid to say something funny. An enormous portion of the writing that has outlived its author—what the world calls literature—has humor in its heart. Shakespeare's darkest tragedies also include his funniest writing. Even the Bible is not above a little risqué slapstick (Genesis 31:32–35, for instance). What your advisers may have in their own hearts is the fear that not everyone can pull it off. That's true. But here is another truth: Humor is a virtue, part of what it means to be human. (The same might be said for sincerity, though more inhumanity seems to have been perpetrated in the name of sincerity than humor.) What to do? The following rule will guide you infallibly: If you think of something funny about your topic, write it down. If you don't, don't.

It's that simple. Trouble arises when an applicant thinks he *should* write something funny or clever to be "different" and then grunts out a noisy and jangling piece that doesn't communicate but calls attention to itself, like a broken toy. Trouble also arises when an applicant thinks he *should* write something solemn or serious to be "safe," and carefully extracts every trace of living tissue from an essay like some ghoulish literary surgeon. What your advisers may not understand is that funny is not the opposite of serious. "Funny," wrote G.K. Chesterton, a very funny essayist, "is the opposite of not funny, and of nothing else." If you see things in a funny way, everything you write will be funny. You can't help it. It's part of you, of your voice.

Admissions officers, like any other readers, are suspicious of something that shows *no* sense of humor. Your essay should show the way you deal with the world every day; though writing can't let someone hear your laugh, your essay should at least hint that you have one.

5

WARMING UP

The hardest thing to do is budge an object from a dead start, particularly if that object is your brain. Once you're in motion, momentum takes over, but sometimes just grunting out those first sentences takes all your strength.

How do you get going? Turn Off the Self-Criticism. Many people, when they begin to write, stop after the first line. "That isn't what I meant," they say, and fuss with a word or phrase. Meanwhile, a big blank page still waits. The temptation to edit before you write is strong, but you can train yourself to resist it. The rewards will be great if you do. Write now, revise later. They are separate steps in the process.

Never outline. Writing outlines at the beginning is like writing postcards home describing the scenery *before* you go on the trip. If you haven't been there yet, how do you know what it's going to be like? There may come a time, after you have written and rewritten, when an outline may help you organize your materials. But first you need some materials to organize.

In the early stages, write everything *fast,* without stopping. Don't worry about coherence yet, or about where to start—just get your thoughts out in whatever crazy pattern they occur. Start anywhere.

That's what professional writers do. Certainly don't worry about me-
chanics or correctness; you'll make cuts and additions later. This is just
stage one. Good writing doesn't spring from people perfect and complete,
like Athena from the forehead of Zeus. You'll need to make at least a few
drafts to get it in shape. How long that takes varies from writer to writer.
You'll get to know your own working schedule, but figure on roughly a
few days per essay—at least.

WHAT DO I HAVE TO SAY?

The answer, of course, is *plenty*. The first step is learning to recognize
what you already know and experience every day, and to see it with new
eyes. It is not an exaggeration to say that every day you gather material for
another college essay.

THE OBSESSION LIST

A writer needs a broad definition of what constitutes an obsession: anything you remember or that pops into your head for no good reason, that
disturbs, elates, provokes, annoys, upsets, inspires, or pulls at you. In only
three minutes or so, try to note at least one item in each category below. (I've added a stimulation here and there.) Nothing is too small. If
you truly draw a blank in a category, just move on. No one needs to see
this—it's just for you. But it's a great source of essays.

- a smell (new playing cards, your aunt's perfume, gasoline, neat's-
  foot oil)
- a word
- a day of the week
- a daily ritual
- a skill or talent you do *not* possess

- a particular sound
- a recurring dream
- a one-time dream
- something about your name
- a place that is too small, secret, or out-of-the-way to have a name (a hollow tree a quarter-mile off the road near the auction house in town, the patch of basil in your mother's garden)
- a small place that has a name (the French Quarter in New Orleans, the corner of Hollywood and Vine, Straus Park)
- a non-obvious body part (skin, freckles, your uncle's ear hair, your own thumbs)
- something a friend once said
- something you wish you had said but didn't
- something you said but wish you hadn't
- an ongoing or unresolved argument you have with someone in particular about something trivial (length of your hair, sister always burning milk in the saucepan)
- an ongoing or unresolved argument about something important (right and wrong, justice, courage, truth)
- your favorite (or least favorite) swear
- something in the natural world (ginko leaf, sparrow, acorn, quartz)
- a building or part of a building
- a human-made visual: an ad, a painting, graffiti
- an accident
- something you read
- a song; a few words from that song
- an image from the Internet
- a piece of dialogue from a movie
- an animal or something about an animal
- a deficit or weakness in yourself
- someone who scared you when you were young

- a metaphor that sticks with you, whether fresh and lively or clichéd
- a cliché
- something about money (Washington's ponytail on the quarter, the color of the ink on the Euro or the yen)
- something about your hair or the hair of others
- something you can't wait for
- a specific, very small moment (lasting no more than a minute) when you knew what love was
- something about elementary school
- something about food (persimmons, Hunan sauce, jawbreakers)
- a fear, small—spiders, multiple choice tests, gefilte fish
- a fear, medium—heights, low-flying planes, clowns
- a fear, jumbo—the expanding universe
- something you did or saw involving fire
- something very specific and particular about water (the tug of a trout at the end of your line, the stink of Tar Ponds in Cape Breton, being blinded by water when your mother doused your head in the tub when you were six)
- something you misunderstood or mispronounced for a long time
- a movie, or some moment in a movie
- a time you had a hand in killing or saving something

THE NOTEBOOK

Use your obsession list to start a notebook of ideas and observations, pieces of conversation and events, and write something in it every day. (OK, twice a week.) It's just a document you can quickly open on a computer—you can even keep it on a cell phone. Keep to a minimum the diary diarrhea: "Saw *her* today. She does not know I exist. She's still going out with that dope," etc. Instead, an essay writer's notebook is a quarry filled with more substantial nuggets that find their way into polished pieces later:

Everything a big bore today. Sat in back row in French. Mr. J's voice like faraway buzzing of bees. Feels good to be almost asleep in class, like a velvet curtain about to come down. Danger, though.

*   *   *

Went to a Mostly Mozart concert last night. Music the usual tinkling. Tiptoe stuff. Good exposure to culture, Mom says. I read somewhere a lot of people die of exposure each year, and I hope I'm not one of them. Slumped over my seat when the lights are turned up. But the hour before the concert is great, sitting on the fountain outside, the sun already gone but still light out. It's cool, and everybody's out, nobody pushing or shoving, just drifting. No rush. Everybody looks lighter.

*   *   *

Someone sent me a chain letter! Fantastic. I don't quite get it, though—something about a South American priest who started it, and it's full of examples of what happens if you don't send it out to twenty friends. Some guy made a million dollars and then lost it the next day and jumped off a building, great stories like that. I wish I had it here. If I send it out I'll be rich soon, it said. Who thinks these things up?

A notebook is a gathering of acorns against an uninspired winter. You may want to show some parts of your notebook to your readers; the material in it can eventually form the backbone of your college essay. It is especially useful as a warm-up before you begin to write something else, but when you get in the habit you'll find yourself making notes at all hours, scribbling away on napkins, bits of newspaper, and other scraps; your muse may not wait for you to sit down at your desk with your Cross pen, but may attack on the bus on the way home, with only an ice cream wrapper handy. An oft-repeated story about Kurt Vonnegut, the novelist, has him beginning his day at work by describing in detail something he saw or experienced that morning, even if only what he had for breakfast, the colors and tastes of something observed; like an appetizer, it gets the juices going.

Your notebook can be a good sounding board for the different voices you want to experiment with. Try imitating other writers. Write as if you were indeed writing to *her* (or *him*). What would you say? (No schmaltz.) Write down all your dreams. Write a full news story of your first memory. If you need more detail for such a story, do what a reporter would do— interview the other witnesses, like your parents, to flesh out the incident. Tell the whole story of your first school day or your first-grade year. Write dialogue: (a) conversations you had or (b) conversations you overheard. Describe your best friend to your worst enemy.

This is your substitute for outlining. Writing is traveling through un-charted territory—your mind. You are the first traveler, and your essays are the world's first maps. So you can't know in advance where you're going. That doesn't mean you don't have a *direction*. But sometimes the direction is marked only by a few big landmarks you can see from where you stand, and taken down in a shorthand like this:

1st dance cl. downtown—HUGE studio, big pipes in the ceiling. My pink warmers, ratty jazz shoes, torn sweatshirt OK. Everybody staring, checking out, is she real? Instr.—dark complexion, high cheekbones—goddess in plastic pants.

There's a difference between note-taking and indiscriminate scrib-bling. Make sure, in your note-taking, that you fill in enough of the sights and sounds and ideas to allow you to recapture your thoughts and see the images when you reread the entry, maybe long afterward. Whenever you can, make sentences.

To find good material for a college essay in your daily life, learn to notice the sometimes small surprises that interrupt the dull procession of yesterdays that threaten to consume all our lives. But fiction sometimes pales in comparison to what's true. "If men would steadily observe realities only," wrote Henry David Thoreau, "and not allow themselves to be deluded, life, to compare it with such things as we know, would be like a fairy tale and the Arabian Nights' Entertainments." Sometimes to write, all you have to do is open your eyes.

STRANGER THAN FICTION

Use your notebook to teach yourself to see. A diary is the record of routine, but the notebook of an essay writer is filled with truths that are Stranger than Fiction. These are the intersections where the remarkable and the ordinary cross paths for a moment. For instance, at the school where I taught we had a guitar teacher named Strum, a swimming coach named Kramp, and an English teacher named Reid. Not to mention a bald teacher named Bauld. All perfect notebook fodder.

Here are some Stranger than Fiction entries from different notebooks:

There's a guy every week who plays an upright piano under the arch in Washington Square Park. It has bright green keys and all the guts of it are exposed. When he finishes, he rolls it away over the cement.

*   *   *

I saw a horse galloping down the middle of the road, without saddle or rider and with reins hanging from his chin. He turned a corner and came head to head with an oncoming car and both braked to a stop, the horse and car both skidding. Driver and horse stopped, looked at each other, and the horse took off in the direction it came, as fast as before.

*   *   *

Today a pickup truck drove up Broadway carrying a huge black sleigh in the back.

Stranger than Fiction is one of the key elements in good essay writing, and the person who goes out with his eyes open for something unusual is likely to find it—again and again. Writing that satisfies keeps coming up with little surprises. But beware the fake surprise, like the observation of a Massachusetts girl that "one minute it was clear and blue, when suddenly the sky was growling and dark with rain clouds." That's not especially surprising in New England, where the weather can change minute by minute. Though "growling" is a nice touch, the surprise and drama of the moment that the writer wants to convey are false. The most common form of false surprise withholds information unnecessarily: "Mr. Pettifoggle was walking down Columbus Avenue minding his own business when It Happened." That's just cheating a reader. Far better and more honest a surprise to write, "When Mr. Pettifoggle was walking down Columbus Avenue minding his own business, a bread truck whipped around the corner and deposited a loaf of pumpernickel at his feet."

RAMBLING AND RANTING

Here's another good warm-up:

Rambling

In ten minutes, write 250 words about everything you're thinking. Keep your reader—friend, brother, teacher—in mind, and write fast, without stopping, and don't worry about shifting topics or ideas. Roam that inner landscape. If you get stuck, look around and write about what you see (sitting near a window is sometimes helpful—the outer landscape), or simply repeat your last line until something new comes to you. If it's good, show it to your reader. If it's disconnected, or boring, or bad, don't worry. This is batting practice. You're just trying to make contact, not hit home runs.

> We went to Boston (family) to see the bar mitzvah of a friend of ours. It was pretty interesting—first one I've ever been to. No chopped liver sculptures or anything. I sort of missed the eighth grade rush at school, arriving a wee bit late. We saw the Renoir exhibit in Boston. Lots of lovely long-haired ladies and blue-eyed children. He's amazing with faces—he paints people I could stare at for hours. But when he sits a girl on a chair, it looks like she's floating a millionth of an inch above it. He just can't seem to get people to sit right in their armchairs. I've never seen so many people in a museum. In class today we talked about an essay I hadn't read. Actually, I read the wrong one. We were talking about hedgehogs and foxes and I read about Tolstoy and the Enlightenment.

It's rambling and fragmented, but there's an honest voice here and sharp details. It's alive. Any of the topics would be worth expanding later and could find their way into a college essay—the first bar mitzvah, reading the wrong essay, museums.

Rambling 2

Try pointing ten minutes of writing toward one topic. If detours appear in your path, follow them, but try to stay generally on course. Write as fast as you can and *don't stop*. Here's a senior remembering an eighth-grade teacher:

> Mr. Thompson carried a light tan leather briefcase with a slightly battered flap and he'd shuffle around in it until he got his papers organized, then he would snap shut the top and we'd see a pile of old yellow faded papers that looked as though they were from around

the period that he was discussing. Then his wrist-breaking lectures began. It's strange the way Mr. Thompson used and handled chalk. He always carried a bunch of colors to draw Greek battle plans with, and each one had a shiny chalk holder because he said he didn't want the chalk to dry out his fingers or make them purple or green. When Mr. Thompson was missing a holder he would never switch them because it would waste too much time. Instead he held the bare chalk with the tips of his fingers, with his pinky raised in the air. It looked like he was waiting for a bird to perch on it.

Here are good details—"wrist-breaking lectures"—and surprising and funny comparisons. Naturally, it's rough. For example, "strange" is a vague word, "make" is weak, "chalk" is overused, and "each one" could refer to battle plans or colors. A few sentences run on. But it's still a lively notebook piece.

You can tell a story in your free writing:

Buses were late this afternoon again. Our bus didn't show at 5:40. 6:00 still nothing. 6:30 Mr. Johnson comes out, tells us well, you see, the buses got stuck, another hour or two, etc. etc. Meanwhile it's Faculty-Trustee dinner night. So Gill and I saunter over and find Coach and Clayton. Mrs. Morris brought us some stuffed mushrooms. Mr. Glasser said, "Hey, no problem, join the party! Here, have something to drink." My respect for him rose rapidly. 7:34 the bus finally arrives. 7:53 around 180th Street, a guy starts running after us shouting, "Yo, yo, you're on fire, yo, you're *on fire!!*" Lance decides this a good enough reason to run around the bus screaming at the top of his fat little lungs. Bus driver stops, gets everyone off the bus, tries to see where the fire is. Decides he better call the company, but lo and behold, buses have no two-way radios. So he jumps on the bus and drives away, presumably to the nearest telephone, leaving forty of us

standing in a rather conspicuous group on the corner. Gill and I say
Bleep this, take a few 9th graders with us and bum a ride on the city
bus. Got home at 8:45. Mom was throwing fits.

Remember, this is just the raw material. But even in dull pieces, one or
two lines will be vivid or memorable. Keep track of them with checks in
the margins or by bracketing or underlining, and soon a higher percentage of good sections will begin to appear. You'll find yourself salvaging
chunks of your ramblings and notebook entries for the foundation of your
college essay.

Free Association

This is more fun with a partner or a group. You both pick the same ordinary object—a dish, a book, a saw, an egg—and really look at it and
think about it. Write the word at the top of a page. Then, in one minute,
make a list of words and phrases the object brings to mind. Make the
list as long as you can in one minute; don't leave anything out. Exchange
lists. Did you have any of the same associations? Although you're bound
to have some overlap, you'll also have wild differences. Each of us has a
personal vocabulary of associations with even the most common things
in our lives—a vocabulary that a writer frequently returns to for material.

Take one association or a series of them that seem connected, and
write fast for fifteen minutes about the object. You might want to praise
it, or attack it, or defend it from people who don't like it, or bring up something new about it that no one ever notices, or tell a story about it. Remember to write for your partner's entertainment.

That's a simple way to collect material to build an essay on—exploring
what you already know. Try it with something that means a lot to you,
like a bicycle or a favorite hat. You might remember how you got the hat,
other hats you've had, why you like hats in general, why you like this hat
in particular, what the point is of wearing a hat at all.

Grousing

Read John Updike's "Beer Can" on page 149. In fifteen minutes, write about something that has changed for the worse during your life. Describe the way it used to be and compare it to the present. If you want, begin with "Consider the——." In a different piece, write about something that has changed for the better.

Boring for Fun

Write fast for ten minutes about the dullest thing you do in the course of a day. Be as detailed as possible. A piece about boredom must be especially lively—don't try to show boredom by creating it. Make a reader feel, for instance, the exquisite torture of sitting through Mr. Snoozleman's lectures on the Punic Wars.

Ranting

Write from anger for ten minutes. Work on one topic or jump around—just keep writing and stay angry.

Your college essay may be buried somewhere in one of these suggestions, waiting to be unearthed. Time to get shoveling.

A FEW WORDS ON WRITER'S BLOCK

This mythic monster, which supposedly devours so much great work before it gets started, is not so ferocious as it is painted. I was tempted to say it doesn't exist at all, but then, in trying to show exactly how it doesn't exist, I got all tangled up and couldn't write a word.

But I'm still a writer's block agnostic; I doubt the existence of the old monster, which was always portrayed as kin to stage fright. I want to change the terms of the discussion. To begin to work, a writer needs to feel the freedom to write badly. Writer's block is nothing more than the loss of this freedom. Somehow, it vanishes. What happens is this: first you start picking over whether to use "but" or "however," when you should be chasing your thoughts across the landscape of your mind; then, very soon—too soon—after you've begun, instead of plunging forward you are crossing out everything you've written that day. Suddenly every sentence you think of is so full of obvious faults that you can't bear even to write one down. The blank page stares at you stupidly, infuriatingly, a reproachful mirror of your own blank mind.

But good writing not only does spring from bad, it must. *Keep going forward*. You can always cross things out later. "I have rewritten—often several times—every word I have ever published," said Vladimir Nabokov, the great novelist. "My pencils outlast their erasers." Writers know they write badly at first. But because we rarely see what's in their wastebaskets, we sometimes forget how badly. Ernest Hemingway said he rewrote the end of *A Farewell to Arms* thirty-nine times.

I'll say it again: first write, no matter how badly; rewrite and edit later. If you feel stuck, use the Rambling device of repeating your last sentence. If that doesn't work, take a ten-minute break: eat an apple, take a shower, play pinball, do squat thrusts. Then come back to it.

Don't expect your first draft to be a masterpiece. In the next chapters you'll see how writing comes alive gradually in the rewriting.

6

COMING ALIVE

Pump life into your essays with a few techniques borrowed from professionals.

TELL A STORY

All the world is not a stage; it's an audience, and it dearly loves a story. Professional writers know this, and use stories and pieces of stories, or *anecdotes,* to bring their work to life. An incident, a bit of conversation, a few vivid characters (real though they be) can make the difference between a lifeless piece and one that sings. Certainly a fragment of dialogue in a college essay—how rare it is!—is like catnip to an admissions officer.

So tell a story in your essay—tell three.

I had never even seen a whole sole before, and there were bones where bones just did not seem to belong. The Charbonneaus (that's what I'll call them) were obviously treating my first night with them as a special occasion—the tablecloth showed fresh creases, there was too much silverware, and the candles that had just been lit were tall and smooth. The only problem was that I really didn't like fish, and the knowledge of how to filet them was not a standard part of the education of a New Jersey girl. But Monsieur and Madame smiled indulgently at me, he with yellow teeth and she with a gold one; I couldn't tell if they meant it or were only making up for Catherine, their daughter, who looked my way as if she might spit.

The candlelight was nice but I wished they had turned the lights on, because romantic semi-darkness and first-time fish fileting were not a good mix. All three of them effortlessly lifted the flesh in one piece off the bone, but I couldn't figure out where to put my fork. And then I realized that I was supposed to use my knife. After I'd broken its back and embedded tiny pieces of bone into the flesh—mine and the fish's—I saw I was losing the battle. So did Catherine, who finally had something to smile about—entertainment tonight, guest starring the American and a badly mauled fish.

Unfortunately I wasn't feeling very funny. I was trying too hard not to seem like another provincial American. Disregarding my first impulse—to deposit my mouthful into the napkin—and my second—to cry—I followed my third instinct and went to the bathroom, trying to make as little fuss as possible.

The night before I left for the Experiment in International Living, my parents had taken me to see *E.T.* As I cried in the backseat on the way home they were quick to say "Don't worry, Niki. If it's really bad you can come home." It was nice of them to say it, but none of us believed it for a minute. When I was in third grade the same two people had made me stick it out at Camp Waziyatah (which, I still remind my parents with satisfaction, folded the next year). I guess some of my tears were for Elliot, the boy in the movie, who had to manage alone in the end. But at least he got to stay home.

Growing up in Tenafly, New Jersey, means that Harold the mailman calls my mother by her first name and all of Bob's Taxi drivers know who lives at 124 Churchill Road; and yes, the sole all comes boneless from the market. Which is to say Tenafly is sheltered, and there isn't much room for developing either independence or filet-manship.

A feeling of security is what you do develop in Tenafly and that feeling comes from living in the comfort of a stable cocoon of famil-iarity. I didn't feel secure in front of Catherine, or even in front of something as harmless as a fish. In fact I felt like an extra-terrestrial and I wanted to go home. But gradually, picking bones out of my teeth in the bathroom, I looked at the big picture. I realized I was not here to learn to debone a fish; Julia Child could have taught me that in my Tenafly living room. Of course, I wasn't sure what I *was* here to do, if anything, but I knew this was part of it.

When I emerged, I saw my dinner lying as I had left it, unroman-tically half-clawed in the candlelight, and for a moment my resolu-tion shook like a weak muscle; I had a quick idea of running out the door and back to the train and the plane and New Jersey. M. Charbon-neau seemed a little puzzled but not especially interested in what-ever dilemma I was having. But his wife looked up sympathetically as I neared the table. "Ça va?" she said.

Out of the corner of my eye, I saw Catherine smirk again.

I sat down. I put a piece of sole on my fork. "Ça va," I said. "Passez du vin, s'il vous plaît."

The I's are frequent, and it's a Trip essay, but this writer gets away with it because she tells a vivid story. She makes us feel the strange new atmosphere by her choice of small details—the parents' teeth, the fish, Catherine's expression. But more than that, the story is clearly going somewhere—not to a moral, but to a point. She doesn't have to tell us "I conquered a difficult experience," because she shows it. She gives us an eye on the experience and spares us the Trumpets of Triumph, or the Marvelous Me Moral. She just tells what happened.

Writing this kind of story is largely a matter of choosing the right incidents, and then letting them speak for themselves. The temptation is always to finish with the sell job, the Trip trap:

"That summer taught me more than ever the importance of learning to get along with many different kinds of people and the necessity of self-reliance. I believe these qualities will be essential in college."

Resist such conclusions at all costs. Events are complicated, and any attempt to squeeze Trumpets of Triumph out of them violates the reader's trust that you must work so hard to build.

The uses of anecdote are many:

a. the introduction and takeoff point for the whole essay.
b. a final note, a story that sums up or crystallizes what you have been saying and leaves a reader with the tone of the whole.
c. a detail in the body of the essay. Anecdotes used this way should not require a big windup. Be economical—save words, save readers.
d. a big story that runs throughout the the essay and shapes the whole. The filetmanship writer sandwiches her thoughts between the pieces of one story—the way movies use flashback technique: she's here in France, then she's back in America at a movie, then she's back again in France.

In a short piece like a college essay, anecdotes are a quick and vivid way to entertain and inform. End with dialogue, like the essay above, or with an action reported. Think like a camera—with what shot do you end the movie that is your essay?

ENTERTAINMENT QUOTIENT

After you have written short sketches like the ones in chapter five and are thinking of rewriting them or expanding them into full-scale college essays, look at them with a critical eye for their Entertainment Quotient:

1. Sense detail. Write to help admissions officers see what you saw, hear what you heard, taste what you tasted. Rather than tell what you learned from photography, show what it looks and feels and even sounds like in a darkroom as your picture emerges—the smell of the chemicals, the red bulb glowing in the darkness. Rather than describe how disciplined you have become as a result of your music lessons, talk about your violin itself, the texture and feel of it, the smell of the rosin and the wood—no one ever thinks of the sense of smell in connection with a violin—details that put a reader through your practice routine with you. Sight, sound, smell, touch, taste. In other words, show what you know.

2. Metaphor. Writers continually see one thing in terms of something else; the result is metaphor, the language of comparison. Sometimes the sheer wit and power of metaphors can carry a piece of writing and make it entertaining and fresh, and learning to think metaphorically is perhaps the most "fun" part of writing. You need to have command of the two common ways of making comparisons. One simply uses "like" or "as": *The leaves are like hands.* The other speaks directly: *The leaves are hands;* or, more subtly, *The leaves beckoned in the wind.* (The metaphor is contained in the verb; leaves don't usually beckon—but they might if they're like hands.) Metaphors are all around you, but through time and use some of them have lost their ability to startle: leg of a chair, face of a clock, eye of a needle. Still others are on their way to the metaphor graveyard but are not quite buried yet. Using them is not the sign of dead metaphor but of a dead mind: white as snow, big as a mountain, high as a kite, smooth as glass. There are thousands of others. To be an entertaining writer you must hammer your own metaphor out of materials you know and understand. A good rule of thumb, suggested by George Orwell, author of *1984*, is never to use a comparison you have heard before.

3. Verbs and Nouns. Nouns are the bones of writing; verbs are the muscles. Entertaining writing gets its structure and strength from them. Don't load up on adjectives—a *"wondrous* evening," a *"multifaceted* personality"—hoping to sound more creative or intelligent. An essay flabby with adjectives only weighs a reader down. Before you can write beautifully you must write well. Try the following:

Without adjectives ("the," "an," and "a" are OK), write a short paragraph or two describing something—a restaurant, a teacher, a pen, a bird, your favorite room in the house—so that it sounds appealing. Then—again without adjectives—make the same subject unappealing. It will seem awkward at first; remember, nothing comes out whole, and it will take a few drafts to trim and tighten the paragraph. But you'll increase your control over words and style. Here's an example:

[1]
There's nothing on the planet like chocolate. Vanilla may be the province of the purist and the test of the connoisseur, but in the kingdom of sweets, darkness rules. Among the garden of edibles, chocolate earns the status of sin—a compliment, like knowledge itself in the Garden of Eden. A silk among desserts, its flavor is like a mixture of malt and nectar and cream.

[2]
People who like chocolate must be in league with dentists, the pokers and pullers who have inherited the reins of torture from the Inquisition. Is chocolate worth the pain? I don't think so. It appeals to chil-

dren who, when the temperature inches up and softens fudge, like to fingerpaint Uncle Nathan's belly with it. It doesn't look like dessert then; it looks more like something the dog deposits. To adults I've seen scrambling for the Toblerone, it's like a drug. Not for nothing is the cacao, from which it is pounded, related to cocaine.

These examples are admittedly freaks. In your final essays you needn't carry adjective-bashing to this extreme, but it's fun to noodle with; this is a true literary pushup that will make your writing stronger.

When you learn to rely on verbs and nouns, they keep you thinking metaphorically, as you can see from the examples. Increasing your store of verbs and nouns opens up that world of comparison. For example, the verb "fasten" might be *pin, stitch, chain, paste, moor, clasp, clamp, suture,* or *belay* (from mountain climbing), depending on the comparison you wanted to suggest. One of my classes found 148 synonyms for the word "walk"—a good many more than are found in any thesaurus. Make a list of your own with a friend or two. Think metaphorically: How does a horse on parade walk? How does a thief walk? A snake? Try the same thing with the word "say."

METAPHOR MADNESS

Children are natural metaphorists. On a walk in the woods in late fall, the four-year-old son of a friend looked up (from his vantage atop his father's shoulders) at all the branches around him losing their leaves and said, "The trees have their pants down."

Kids are always reporting what they see in fresh language; they haven't learned how to be dull. We grow up into dullness, just the way we lose the imaginary friends that we sometimes had as kids. But kids don't know what they're saying and can't build on it; with them, metaphor is simple habit, part of the way they think. In one sense, learning to write is learning to recover the freshness and imagination of kid talk and harnessing it to grown-up consistency.

You can help redevelop the metaphorical habit by doing what kids (and writers) do—playing games. I call one Fruits and Vegetables, a good one for long car or train rides with friends or family. To start, the one who's "it" thinks of a person you all know, like a figure from history, a teacher, or a neighbor, and says only "a teacher" or "historical female." The others must try to guess who it is by asking metaphorical questions: "What kind of vegetable would he be?" You must respond with an answer that in your mind reflects the essence of the person, not just a superficial characteristic. For example, don't answer "red pepper" simply because the subject has red hair. Better to answer pepper if the subject has a spicy and colorful personality. Questioners should really stretch—which type of bird would he be, which highway in America, which breakfast food, which household appliance. Each guesser is allowed only one guess before he is out, but there is no limit to the number of questions.

Here's another good metaphor game for those long rides. I call it Raymond Chandler, in honor of the mystery writer known for his similes. You may need pencil and paper at first, but soon you'll be able to play it in your head. Begin with two columns of nouns, one concrete, the other abstract. For example:

hammer	honesty
piano	love
light bulb	trust
birdseed	disappointment
rowboat	tension

Your friend picks one word from column A, one from B, and both of you make a sentence that shows why they're alike: Love is like a light bulb:

you can turn it off and on. Or, Love is like a rowboat: it takes hard work to keep it moving forward. Or, Love is like a piano: you have to practice to be good. Writers are constantly indulging this playfulness with ideas and words, and the metaphors, forced as they are, sometimes uncover strange truths you never saw before.

Play the same game with things you care about:

> soccer
> books
> college
> teachers
> sleep

Match them with nouns at random: shirt, glass, key, tiger, dinner.

Robert Frost, the poet, played this game. "Poets," he said, "are like baseball pitchers. Both have their moments. The intervals are the tough things." So did E. B. White: "A writer is like a bean plant—he has his little day, and then gets stringy."

Don't worry about stretching it to ridiculous limits—that's how you get better and better at seeing connections and playing with ideas.

B. S. DIGRESSION

"C'mon, Mr. B, that's b.s.," my students sometimes snicker when we play these games. "Everything can't be like everything else." (Actually, when you look closely enough—at the level of particle physics, say—everything *is* almost *exactly* like everything else. Metaphor is not just a poetic fancy.) But I couldn't agree more; it is b.s. And inferior b.s. is a very shoddy product, adulterated with twigs, stones, and debris. But pure b.s. is a noble, fertile resource; stuff *grows* in it.

Students give b.s. a bad name. Here's how: For the upcoming essay-test on the Civil War, you lock down and study like a dog all weekend, learning every strategy and body count, and the exact blood-alcohol level of Ulysses S. Grant at the battle of Vicksburg. Your classmate, Bartleby the Slacker, never cracks a book, and you happen to know he spent a good portion of the weekend imitating Grant's leisure rather than memorizing battle plans. You sit for the essay. Mr. Snoozleman reveals the topic: How did the South lose the war?

When you get the essay back (you already know where I'm taking this), you get the B, Bartleby gets the A. *But he just* b.s.*'ed his way through that*, you sputter, *and Snoozleman* bought *it*. Yes. I urge you to cultivate that skill as soon as you can and with as much care as you can muster. When b.s. reaches a certain (very high) level it is called *thinking*, and when it finds a voice, it is called literature. (Ever wonder why in the one high school class you have to take every year, and therefore apparently the main vehicle of education, the material consists mainly of a bunch of b.s.—at school it's called fiction and drama, but in my neighborhood it's called *lies*.)

The college essay, reduced to its essentials: b.s. and memory.

DIGRESSION ON MEMORY

You are not what you eat but what you remember. Our fascination with amnesia stories in movies and literature is that we know identity begins and ends in memory. It's the unique source no one else has, the foundation of what only you can write.

Luckily, your memory is b.s.-ing you constantly. You know this if you've discussed with your parents a cherished early memory—that time you fell off your new red tricycle at your grandmother's and had to go to the hospital, for example. "Actually," your mom says, "it was your sister's silver scooter, and it was at the park, and you didn't go to the hospital for that but you did go a bit later, for the ear tubes. . . ."

This truth about point of view drives the police nuts. Four eyewitnesses to a crime cannot agree on the number of bank robbers, or what the crooks looked like, wore, or said.

If you spend any time with the elderly, you see how memory changes; your grandmother can't remember what she had for lunch or what grade you're in, but she can vividly recall capsizing in a canoe at camp when she was ten.

Your memory is not the truth of *then*; it's your story—your b.s., your fiction, your drama—of who you are now. The writer's confidence is this: My memory selects for a reason, and I write to discover, or b.s. my way toward, that reason.

So you can b.s. your memory right back.

If you wanted to start an essay right now you could think of your very first memory. (Sometimes when I do this in workshops, some touching innocent will say—and mean it—"I can't remember." And I'll have to say, "Start with breakfast today and work backward.") Maybe it will be a fragment from when you were three or four, just an image. See it in your mind's eye, the colors, the sounds, the moment. Now realize how little else you remember of that year when you were four—365 days' worth, like every other year. Ask yourself: why do I remember that, of all things? (The writer's answer: because it's important to your story of yourself *now*.) And then: *how* is that about me now? Your essay is the great-b.s. answer to that question. Everyone could begin an essay with exactly the same phrase and the resulting pieces would be as individual and identifiable as fingerprints. And that phrase is *When I was six . . .*

7

SWEETHEART,
GET ME REWRITE!

In old movies, the grizzled reporter at the scene of the crime—the leg man—races to a pay phone and shoves in his nickel. "Sweetheart," he rasps when the gum-popping receptionist answers in the newspaper office, "get me rewrite!" Then he barks a few garbled facts to a team of rewrite specialists who turn out something snappy and readable. *Time* magazine still works essentially this way. Wouldn't it be great to shout a few thoughts into a telephone and a day later have a college essay come back? But it's unlikely that you have a staff of people wearing sleeve guards and green eyeshades poised in your living room waiting to punch up your copy. Sweetheart, you *are* rewrite.

Writers revise in different ways. I have a friend, a novelist, who rewrote the entire draft of his book three times from beginning to end, by hand, on heavy paper with fine fountain pens. He is insane. Many write a draft directly on the computer, then print a copy to attack with a pen, adding phrases and sentences, crossing out, making notes and arrows. Others still use scissors and tape to move paragraphs around. Some write and revise completely on the computer. I know students who write on their instant messaging devices—what we used to call "phones." Only by writing and rewriting often will you find the method of revision that works best for you.

Whatever your method, you know it's revision time when you've written a few pages and your draft begins to dull, like a knife in constant use. You're near the end, but suddenly you can't cut through the jungle of your thoughts, and you need to stop. It's important to keep writing fast until you've pushed a topic as far as it will go. But when you revise, things slow down a bit—not as slow as in the final editing, but a clear change in tempo from your draft. At the rewrite stage, keep an essay alive by pausing to ask the right questions of yourself.

WHERE AM I?

You can teach yourself to be your own rewrite department. One way to find out where you are is to identify good lines. Always work initially from what's good. Also try writing down on a separate sheet the most important nouns and verbs in your draft. Reread all the metaphors. What do they suggest? These are just tricks to help you be aware of the landmarks you've left scattered around, in case you don't know where to go. Often, simply reading your draft carefully will be enough to plot the course ahead.

Can you find a main idea, reducible to a sentence or two, that can serve as your compass? What's the story behind the story? Rereading his first draft, the writer in chapter four who lamented the passing of the sixties might have summed up his idea this way: "Let's not bury the sixties yet—at least not while I'm around."

You may find that a detour you took makes a better essay. Follow it. Or you may want to get back on your original course. Once you glimpse an idea in the distance again, think about rearranging your draft to plot the best way to get there. Sometimes that means a straight line, sometimes the scenic route. It helps to imagine that the path of your idea, like a forest trail seen from an airplane, creates (in your mind and a reader's) a *shape*.

WHAT SHAPE AM I IN?

All essays have shape, or form—not on the page, where they look alike, but in the mind, where they differ sharply. A point-by-point logical argument may climb down to its conclusion like steps; a humorous essay may sprout crazy petals from a center. An anecdotal piece may swerve briefly away from its main subject in an S-curve and finally point, as the tail of an S does, back to the beginning. Talking about shape this way is metaphorical, not literal, but readers sense the pattern (whether or not they realize it), and it puts them on firm footing.

Shape often comes *after* the first draft. You may have only a vague notion of shape—or none at all—as you begin, but it will gradually emerge from the writing, like a figure from a sculptor's block. You may find that what you have to say is shaped by the flow of one memory or experience, like the student essay on the stepmother in chapter eleven; several smaller anecdotes may give it form, as in David Owen's "Pfft," in chapter twelve. Sometimes the shape begins to grow out of your revisions of the beginning and the end.

One way of looking at shape is to think about the time sequence. Look at an essay like George Orwell's "Shooting an Elephant," and assign a number to every change in its chronology or dating: 1 = the earliest incident mentioned (not as it appears in the *text*, but as it happened in *time*), 2 = the next, and so on in order until the latest. Orwell does not go in order, but jumps all over the place chronologically. So what *is* his organizing principle?

Then number your own draft, and play around with the order, discovering your own organization. The "frustrated cowgirl" essay on page 136, for example, goes something like this: 6, 2, 1, 3, 5, 4, 7, 6 (or, roughly, the move to NY; her birth; her dad's coming to Oregon; second grade; sixth grade; back to earlier grades; current perspective; and back to the NY move—or 1979, '67, '63, '74, '78, '76, '85, '79).

THE BEGINNING: HOW (AND WHEN)

Earlier I urged you to "start anywhere" when you begin to write a draft.
Still true. But once you've written a couple of pages you need to think
about what newspapers call a *lead,* which rhymes with seed, which is the
function of your first sentence—to plant early in a reader's mind something that will bear fruit later. The worst thing a lead can be is *leaden,*
which rhymes with deaden, which describes what a careless or dull lead
does to readers and to your application. If your writing has only one
chance to sparkle, it should sparkle at the beginning.

The irony about a good lead is that it is very often written *last.* That's
right. It's frequently a product of revision. That's partly because (I repeat)
writers don't usually know what they're going to say until they say it.
Leads come last also because they're tough to do and they matter so much.
Even the best writers stumble forward with a kind of prayer: Maybe one
will come to me. And when they work at it enough, one usually does.

Some experienced writers do keep their eyes open for a lead as they
write the draft. This is tricky. Working under frequent deadlines, a journalist tries to find shortcuts, and working from a good lead gives the draft
an immediate focus and often does away with the need for a lot of revision. But that's in the hands of those who do it for a living, every day. You
can try it too, with this warning: The minute you slow down and start
groping instead of writing fast, forget about the lead and push ahead.

Now and then, when you're really cooking, you will whip up a good
lead right at the outset. If it comes, fine; if it doesn't, don't worry about it.
Say to yourself, I'll write a lead if it's the last thing I do. It may be.

What is a good lead? For writers, a line or two that gives a shaping
edge, an "angle," to an essay; for readers, something that nudges them
into the rest of the piece. That's really all—something to stir up a reasonable amount of curiosity. Here's the first line of George Orwell's essay on
England during World War II: "As I write, highly civilised human beings

are flying overhead, trying to kill me." Only the subverbal would not read on. A *great* lead is something else—a memorable sentence in itself and the distilled essence of the essay. E. B. White began "Death of a Pig," perhaps the only good Pet Death essay ever written, with this: "I spent several days and nights in mid-September with an ailing pig and I feel driven to account for this stretch of time, more particularly since the pig died at last, and I lived, and things might easily have gone the other way round and none left to do the accounting." There's a seed lead for you—it contains the wry humor of the rest of the piece, a summation of the narrative, and a glimpse of the main idea: that the reminders of our own deaths are tragic and comic both.

A bad lead is all windup and no pitch: "In the following essay I hope to show . . ." Just *do* it, don't announce it. Or a false question: "Have you ever thought about bee pollen?" You know perfectly well your readers haven't thought about bee pollen. The false question rings hollow.

Here are a few leads you might play with:

The Anecdote

Probably the most common beginning for an essay. As you saw in chapter six, a story or a snippet of dialogue is an extremely effective lead—as long as it bears on your topic. One girl began an essay about her father, "Every Sunday I wake up to a 1940s Prell Shampoo jingle sung in falsetto by a short, wiry, balding intellectual. My dad is a nut." Watch for anecdotal leads in newspaper features and magazine stories, and pay attention to how they work.

The Why? Lead

When the reader asks Why? In response to your lead, you're in business. "I try to live reasonably in the modern world, but it gets harder and harder." Why? In another of his essays, George Orwell begins, "In Moulmein, in Lower Burma, I was hated by large numbers of people—

the only time in my life that I have been important enough for this to happen to me." Why?

The Paradox

The only sound worth hearing is silence. A paradox is an apparent contradiction that is somehow true. Once you get in the habit, these will come easily, and they are very stimulating to your essay writing (and thought!) and a great way to begin. *Nothing is more serious than humor. The most practical thing you can do is dream. It is difficult to tell the truth with facts. Intelligence is the one thing IQ tests do not measure.*

The Shocker

For instance, "I do some of my best thinking in the bathroom" (p. 141). Nobody could pass up the rest of that essay. It's good to startle readers now and then. "I grew up a killer," might begin a light story of becoming a vegetarian.

But the Shocker is not simply any wild or fanciful statement; abused, it's just another tabloid headline. A good one steers a reader to the main idea of the essay. Use it like the loaded weapon it is, with care.

The Curmudgeon

A curmudgeon is a contrary person; the Curmudgeon lead is ornery, sometimes a paradox. "*Moby-Dick* may be a great book, but it is not a good book." You can skewer an immense number of conventional ideas if you're good at the Curmudgeon lead. Here's one by G. K. Chesterton (from around 1907): "I have no sympathy with international aggression when it is taken seriously, but I have a certain dark and wild sympathy with it when it is quite absurd." It doesn't have to be a paradox, though, as this lead from H. L. Mencken (curmudgeon of all curmudgeons) shows: "No man ever quite believes in any other man."

The Split

You can divide people or things into a few simple types. "There are those who have faith in man-made things and those who do not," wrote Ellen Goodman (p. 153). Ada Louise Huxtable began an article called "Modern-Life Battle: Conquering Clutter," with this: "There are two kinds of people in the world—those who have a horror of a vacuum and those with a horror of the things that fill it." Both writers may have been thinking of Charles Lamb's lead (almost 160 years ago): "The human species, according to the best theory I can form of it, is composed of two distinct races, the men who borrow, and the men who lend." It's a good device for a light essay. But always stay close to your own experience. The whole point of beginning this way is that you, too, fall into one of the categories, usually the apparently inferior one.

The Raymond Chandler

Simply use a comparison like one of those from the game in chapter six. "The allurement that women hold out to men," begins a Mencken essay, "is precisely the allurement that Cape Hatteras holds out to sailors: they are enormously dangerous and hence enormously fascinating."

The Confession

David Owen's first sentence (p. 155), for example. The Confession lead is not *really* confessional—the aim isn't to reveal intimate details from a sense of guilt. You're trying to entertain, remember. (p. 141)

"I do some of my best thinking in the bathroom" is a Confession and a Shocker both. What makes the Confession lead effective is the honesty of the observation. By opening up a subject that you know other people—in Owen's case, people his age or older—recognize but don't talk about, you take the reader into your confidence.

Stating the Obvious

I mean the obvious that is hidden, because it is right under our noses. In the lead to "Heavier than Air" (p. 147), White highlights the *weight* of a plane, something so obvious we never think about it. The essay is structured around the simple idea that a plane is *big*. The planes in George Orwell's lead are different from White's, though Orwell states the obvious in an equally startling way—of *course* the people flying a plane are highly civilized; *naturally* they are trying to kill him—there's a war on. But the line is striking, and makes us realize something we knew-but-didn't-know. A good Stating the Obvious lead might be something as simple as "San Francisco is a long way from New York." Well, now that you mention it, of course it is. Why do you bring it up?

Refer to this list—sketchy as it is—during revision, or make up variations of your own. I'll refer to it, too, when I get around to writing the introduction to this book. Maybe something will come to me.

ENDINGS

Let's look at the other pole. Once you hook readers, you've got to make sure to land them. Here's how you *don't* finish a piece: "in conclusion," "in summation," "finally," "I would like to close by saying," or any of the other staples from the Stylebook of the Dead.

The best endings remember where they came from, but they don't insult readers by calling attention to themselves or repeating what's already been said. Beginnings and endings *speak* to each other. "I do some of my best thinking in the bathroom" ends "Maybe they'd think of something." Even the sounds are alike: some thinking, think of something. Another of the Exhibits in chapter eleven (p. 126): "Except for my struggle with jacks—I could never get past sixies while Leslie Ackerman whizzed through tenzies and back to onezies all in one turn—this application is the greatest challenge I've faced." The end: "The whole thing makes sevenzies look easy."

The pros know the same secret. "This seems to be an era of gratuitous inventions and negative improvements," is Updike's lead on page 149, and his ending speaks to it: "What we need is Progress with an escape hatch."

Because of the close relationship between the beginning and the end, you may find yourself working on both of them simultaneously; in my magazine writing I have often discovered a good lead buried in what I originally thought was the ending.

Another way to end effectively is with an anecdote, as David Owen does (p. 155) in his piece about growing older. The quoted sound from his father—not even a word!—is surprising and memorable because it sums up so succinctly everything Owen himself has been feeling about growing older. Owen is here using a favorite device of reporters—letting someone else say what's also on the writer's mind.

I don't know for sure, but I'm guessing that Owen started with the quotation from his father—it goes back further in time than anything else he talks about—and wrote the rest of the piece "into" it. You can work the same way. Write your last sentence first—a strong line or two of dialogue—and then write the essay it completes.

Ending with a good quotation often gives a feeling of finality. The filet-frightened New Jersey girl in chapter six quotes herself and leaves us to judge from that how she handled her problem. In both her essay and David Owen's, we say the end-feeling works because the *rhythm* is good. Rhythm in writing refers to the length of sentences, which, in any good piece, should vary. Almost any rhythm, handled well, can work for the ending, but there are certain patterns that writers continually call on, just as there are final cadences and chords in a song or a symphony that let you know the music is ending. Many writers find the sound of finality in short sentences. Owen, Russell Baker (p. 150), Ellen Goodman (p. 153), and a few of the best student pieces in chapter eleven end with short, vigorous sentences. Especially effective endings often set up the last line with a long, slow sentence full of commas and twists of thought, followed by one or two short, brisk lines to close. Try it. (See?)

One warning about finishing with an anecdote or quotation. Make sure it bears closely on your main point. There are few things more confusing than an irrelevant story. If David Owen had ended his piece this way, it would have fallen flat:

> When my daughter and I were walking in the park recently, she bent to pick a yellow flower by the side of the path. "Look," she said, clutching the daisy and holding it out to me. "It's the sun."

There's nothing wrong with this story; it just doesn't complete the thought he's been developing.

In a college essay, the end is not quite as important as the beginning, but make sure your ending remembers where it came from and sounds final.

Hearing Your Own Voice: Revising Style

Your writing voice—the sound of your sentences—is your "style." It's a combination of your word choice, tone, and even your thought. But many individual styles fall into a few big divisions. Compare:

A. Please elaborate upon the circumstances surrounding the collision.
B. Describe the accident.
C. How'd you crash the car?
D. What went down with your ride?

Four different ways of saying the same thing—four different voices. All can be the same serious, dispassionate tone, but the style is different.

A is formal—tuxedo talk. Scholars, lawyers, and people seeking to maintain a professional distance from their audience use it.

B is informal—a sweater, comfortable shoes. The voice is direct and unadorned.

C is colloquial—T-shirt and sneakers, the breeziness of everyday conversation.

D is slang—flip flops, street talk.

We slip in and out of these styles as we talk, and in your first draft you'll probably find pieces of different styles. Good. In your first draft you are just getting the words out and should write in the voice that feels most comfortable. In revising, you must decide whether each shift in style is effective.

Work toward the informal. It is the most flexible voice, one that can be serious or light. On top of that bass line, you can play variations—just as you do with rhythm. Professional writers mix them skillfully, sometimes in a single sentence:

> This seems to be an era of gratuitous inventions and negative improvements. Consider the beer can.

The first line is strictly tuxedo, the second a plain pullover.

> Even by standards of that time it was a primitive place. There was no electricity. Roads were unpaved. In our house there was no plumbing. The routing of summer days was shaped by these deficiencies.

Four sweaters followed by a little hint of tails and top hat.

Dialogue usually wears T-shirt or flip flops; few people speak with the directness of an informal style or the elevated sound of the formal.

> Rising dust along the road from the mountains signaled an approaching event. A car was coming. "Car's coming," someone would say.

Baker puts them back to back. "A car was coming. 'Car's coming.' "

When you reread your draft, be alert for shifts in your style—are these changes of dress effective, or should you be returning to your informal wardrobe? Although in your essays you should stay close to the informal, good writing moves back and forth easily among the different styles. In general steer clear of tuxedo talk—to write well in a formal style takes years. On the other hand, too much slang in an essay grates like too many car horns in traffic. You're looking for balance. One object of revision is to decide when you should go casual and when you should dress up, and to wear it all convincingly.

8

TINKERING

It's not always easy to say where rewriting (the Big Stuff) leaves off and editing (the Small Stuff) begins. For instance, I talk about style as Big Stuff and tone as Small, but the distinction, I confess, is almost arbitrary. As you'll see in chapter nine, an essay *evolves*, and the stages often blur. You probably won't be able to resist some tinkering when you rewrite. Like an auto mechanic, you'll notice a few small parts out of whack and start pulling here, twisting there, jiggling this connection, tightening that one, to make your prose engine run better, while a big problem in the exhaust system still waits. There's nothing wrong with that. We'd all like to be more organized, but we aren't. That goes double for writers.

Still, if you're going to be a good mechanic and not just another slob banging away with a wrench, it helps to have some idea what you're doing. There is value in remembering the separation of draft, rewrite, and edit. It can keep you from fussing with details when you should be thinking about what you're trying to say. Imagine the stages as different speeds in that vehicle you're fixing: Draft is overdrive, whipping along so fast the view is a blur—you're just trying to hold on around the corners; rewrite is travel gear, steady but slower, good for seeing the whole panorama; and editing is a stop-and-go crawl that gives you every bit of scenery in detail for as long as you want.

A good college essay—or any piece of writing—needs careful editing to develop. Just as you can learn to be your own rewrite department, you can be your own best editor.

TONE: HOW TO WIN FRIENDS AND INFLUENCE ADMISSIONS OFFICERS

Tone, in writing and speaking, is the same—your *mood*. Admissions officers read your essay to discover the "type of person" you are, and your mood is one very transparent clue. Learn to control the tone of your writing voice the way you control the tone of your speaking voice; you wouldn't want your boy- or girlfriend to think you were bitter or sarcastic when you felt friendly and forgiving. That's how misunderstandings start, and you can't kiss and make up with admissions officers.

Remember your audience. Would you boast at a party to someone you were attracted to—"Hi, I've really made myself a better person lately. I really know how to handle challenges"? Unlikely—unless you wanted to test how fast he or she could politely find someone else to talk to. Don't boast in your essay. Many students do, on the mistaken premise that they must sell themselves.

Don't whine. "I have some teachers who are mean, but others are all right." Don't plead. "I think First Choice is a great school and I've really wanted to go there for as long as I can remember." Pleaders are described by admissions officers as "sweaty." Controlling your tone means being sensitive to the effect of your words on a reader. Compare three possible lines you might use to explain poor performance in one class:

    A. I can't stand physics.
    B. Physics is a stupid science.
    C. Physics is a mystery to me.

All may represent the truth as you see it, and you might say any one of them to a close friend who forgives you your little peeves. But which would you use with Mr. Quark, the physics teacher, sitting across from you? The tone of A is aggressive, and B insulting. At least C, which expresses an honest humility, gives you a chance of being heard without raising the teacher's hackles. Change the audience again. Which is best for talking to that hypothetical person I keep bringing up—someone you are attracted to but don't know well? (Specifically, you don't know whether he or she is a physics wiz. And you *really* want to get to know this person better.) A *could* work—but it would have to precede a pretty entertaining rap to be winning. B is out of the question—whiny and dumb. C in this case could express awe and wonder—your best bet to sound like an interesting person.

What kind of tone should you use in your college essay? Whatever suits you. Even stubborn can work, if you know you're stubborn and don't take yourself too seriously. A writer doesn't pick his tone from a menu— "I think I'll be bittersweet today, because I plan to be ironic tomorrow." The mood grows out of the subject and the writer's authentic feeling about it. But a writer learns to recognize through practice what sounds right, just as you have developed an instinct for the right way to talk to different friends. If you try to sound friendly and you don't feel that way, it always sounds fake—to you and, you can be sure, to your audience.

But there is no fail-safe tone that will prevent you from bombing. I could say that admissions officers always like a tone that is Nice-and-Friendly, or Respectful, or Enthusiastic. It would make sense, but it wouldn't be entirely accurate. *Trying* to sound Nice or Respectful or Enthusiastic, like trying to be funny or clever, doesn't work. For one thing, Nice and Respectful turn easily into Boring and Sweaty, and Enthusiastic into Fluffy. Admissions officers will like who you are if you give them— and yourself—a chance. Remember the natural voice. You can only be who you are and have the moods you have. Concentrate on using your moods to produce something entertaining and revealing.

Read your draft aloud—in what tone of voice would you say your lines? What do your chosen readers have to say about it? The good thing about writing is that if it sounds whiny or brittle or just plain fake, you can change it. Just like that.

DICTION

Diction is word choice, one source of tone. A dictionary, one source of words, nourishes a writer. A thesaurus, on the other hand—a list or a book of synonyms without definitions—can be a cauldron of artificial flavorings. Words extracted from the thesaurus (and not organically grown from your reading) may sound good. But artificial flavorings can also cause disease, and people who know the anatomy of prose can easily see the cancerous lumps forming in your writing. Too many college essays are choked with "myriad"s, "plethora"s, and other test-tube words:

> A student's scholastic experience encompasses a multitude of endeavors.

Yecch. It's not entirely your fault—this elephantiasis of the word infects more than college essays. Even baseball players (and announcers), usually so vivid, have caught it: a pitcher no longer throws "heat" or "smoke," he now "has good velocity." This is plain bad, an attempt by insecure people to sound educated. Velocity certainly doesn't sound any faster than speed—we don't talk about something moving at "the velocity of light," which is a good deal quicker than even MLB's best. (Physics teachers tell me that, technically, velocity and speed aren't even interchangeable, though baseball people don't know that.) Perhaps because players today earn astronomical salaries, they think they deserve more expensive words to describe their pitches. But inflated language doesn't make the fastballs any faster; it just makes the speaker sound pretentious and dumb. Get good value from your words.

By all means *learn more words*—by reading more, and by listening to people who speak clearly and vividly. That's the only way you'll understand how to use them. (Nobody—no *writer*—learns words from vocabulary lists.) Sometimes it means training your ear to distinguish the lively from the flat when both come from the same source. Ballplayers today, for instance, also say a pitcher "can bring it," or "throws gas," two vivid metaphors.

Another way to build your cache of words is to learn the exact names of things you touch and see every day. For instance, here are some words that name common parts of a house: cornice, dormer, gable, widow's walk, garret, wing, gutter, shutter, rafter, clapboard, eave. Though you probably see these architectural details every day, how many of them do you recognize by name? Knowing—and using—the names for the parts of a boat, of a church, of a flower, of a cow, of everything around you, helps your language come alive.

One suggestion: In your word researches, lean toward the plain and solid word where you have a choice between it and a more scientific-sounding one; of the two words for a dolphin's nose, for example, *beak* is more vigorous than *rostrum,* and the implied comparison with birds even catches something of a dolphin's playfulness.

Good writing knows the names of things, and good words are accurate and lively. I guarantee that if you are reading this book, you already know enough words to write a good essay.

But even among familiar words, not all are created equal. A few have come to mean so little—not only in college essays (though especially there) but also in memos, letters, speeches, and conversation—that they are almost meaningless. These you must un-learn:

interpersonal	commitment
interact	leadership (and "leadership
responsibility	role")
excellence	individual (in place of
integrity	*person*)
diversity	objective (as noun)
situation	aspect
relationship	factor
bottom line	endeavor
utilize	tendency
values	considerable
achievement	
dedication	

There are many more, and I don't even have room for empty phrases like "at the present time" (which should be simply "now" or "today"). Many applicants use these puffs of smoke in a wrong-headed effort to appear intelligent and worthy of admission. But language like this is the hallmark of people who have nothing to say and usually know it. "I have come to admire and respect him," wrote one New York politician of another recently, "for his commitment to values we all cherish in American life." The words are like incense, filling the air with pretty-smelling smoke that drowns every whiff of the sharper, less pleasant odor of truth. Which values? How does he know we *all* "cherish" them? Who's we? Can someone be committed to values? What does that mean?

Some of the words on my list are bad because they are jargon, like *bottom line*. Some are pretentious, like *utilize* and *individual*. Some are so vague we never know what their purpose is in a sentence: *situation, aspect, commitment*. Like so many feathers, these words just take up space and insulate us from meaning. Others have been degraded by dishonesty and overuse: *integrity, excellence, responsibility*, words so often used to describe criminals, incompetence, and evasiveness that they make literate people laugh. They are almost always used to manipulate an audience, not communicate. Here are other smoke balls:

obviously	virtually
clearly	unquestionably
rather	particularly
somewhat	relatively
kind of, sort of	

It's cheating to begin a paragraph with "Clearly. . . ." If it is clear, don't say so; just show it and stop stacking the deck against the reader. If it is not clear—which it usually isn't when "Clearly . . ." raises its beguiling head—then saying so is dishonest. *Clearly, obviously, unquestionably* are loaded dice intended to cheat the reader.

I was kind of tired.

Megan is rather opinionated.

That's a somewhat risky endeavor.

More cheating, here from cowardice rather than emptiness or deception. Don't waffle. If you have something to say, say it: I was tired. Megan is opinionated. That's risky.

Clearly, in the rush of your draft you will use many words that don't pull their weight. Obviously, you can revise out all sloppiness, all smoke screens, all cheating. Unquestionably, you will write a better essay if you do.

TRANSITIONS

Writing transitions is the art of getting from here to there and back in your thoughts without jolting readers out of their seats. (Though sometimes you *want* to jolt them.) An essay is like a chain. Each link (idea, anecdote, description) is complete in itself and yet is also part of the one before and the one after. Many of the usual devices for connecting parts of an essay are useful and quick if not skillful: *but, instead, now, later, then.* But others are clanky: *nevertheless, therefore, moreover, in addition, thus, more important, secondly* (and *thirdly*), *finally,* and other formal, archaic-sounding words.

Sometimes you can't avoid the ordinary devices. Updike, the least clanky of writers, calls on them in making transitions in "Beer Can": although he shifts simply from present to past with the use of "was" in his third sentence, he brings back the present with "Now we are given, instead." Then "However" and "But" take us into the future. Because the shifts are quick, the words do not call attention to themselves, and we hardly notice the transitions at all. That's the goal.

In "Summer Beyond Wish" (p. 150), Russell Baker doesn't even try to make smooth transitions. He moves from scene to scene like a filmmaker, in sharp cuts. He can do this because he's arranged his images in gradually increasing importance and because he's followed the sequence of a day—morning images first, then afternoon, and then evening.

Transitions connect or contrast time or thought. Sketch the big movements of your essay, the way an artist suggests with a few broad strokes the main shapes in his composition. Is the piece an If . . . but no . . . therefore essay? Or is it in two sections, Once . . . but now? Or a simple time sequence: This . . . then this . . . then this? There are as many formats as there are essays. Charting the main transitions in your draft can help you polish its shape.

TRIMMING THE FAT: AN ABSURDLY BRIEF GUIDE

Many college essays are bloated with sentences that could be tightened or completely eliminated. When you've got only five hundred words—and often fewer—to nourish readers, every one must count.

In other words, *simplify*. Here are ways to reduce the most unsightly sentence fat.

1. *Who, which, that,* and *what* often swell a sentence with blubber. Use them only when necessary.

FAT:

Uncle Nathan is someone who cares only about fly fishing.

TRIM:

Uncle Nathan cares only about fly fishing.

FAT:

Todd had a dog which he took on long walks.

TRIM:

Todd took his dog on long walks.

FAT:

What Betty hoped was that the president would admit a mistake.

TRIM:

Betty hoped the president would admit a mistake.

2. *There* and *it* are often unnecessary.

FAT:

There were geese swimming on the pond.

TRIM:

Geese swam on the pond.

FAT:

It is the love of fly fishing that keeps Uncle Nathan going.

TRIM:

Love of fly fishing keeps Uncle Nathan going.

FAT:

At the end of the play there was a groan from the audience.

TRIM:

At the end of the play the audience groaned.

3. Be alert for fatty uses of the word *thing*.

FAT:

The thing I'm interested in is science.

TRIM:

I'm interested in science.

4. Trimming *thing* in that example also allowed me to cut *is*. Lazy uses of *is, am, were, was, are,* and the other forms of the verb *to be,* can cause ugly sentence spread.

FAT:

Fifty years ago, it was natural for athletes to play before adoring crowds.

TRIM:

Fifty years ago, athletes expected to play before adoring crowds.

FAT:

In a telephone survey it was shown that there is little support for secret operations.

TRIM:

A telephone survey revealed little support for secret operations.

The verb *to be* is not always so expendable. But be careful with it. Check your drafts to make sure every use of *to be* pulls its own weight.

5. Cut *second helpings*. When you're trying to get your prose into shape, needless restatements overstuff a sentence.

FAT:

My brother is an honest person. That's a quality I respect in him.

TRIM:

I respect my brother's honesty.

We know honesty is a quality and your brother is a person.

Try cutting out the second helpings in this paragraph:

A piano is a temperamental thing. The unpredictable nature of this instrument is apparent to anyone who has an old one, as we do. My mom's big upright has good days, when it sounds like a concert grand. It also has bad days, when the keys become stiff or sticky as a result of slight changes in humidity, and it never quite acts the same under different conditions. It's often as stubborn as a mule. When the temperature is colder, the tone has a harder character than when it is warm. At these times it makes sounds more like something being tortured.

Double helpings: We know a piano is a thing. "The unpredictable nature of this instrument" treads the same ground as the first sentence. "It never quite acts the same under different conditions" is completely unnecessary. A rewrite might look like this:

An old piano is as temperamental as a mule. On good days my mom's big upright sounds like a concert grand. But when the humidity changes quickly, the keys stiffen and stick and the tone hardens, and it whines and groans as if tortured.

6. *Replace vague verbs.* Verbs are the muscles of writing. *Become, get, do, make,* and *have* can be weak; they don't generate motion or action. Reread the two paragraphs above.

WEAK:

the keys become stiff or sticky

STRONG:

the keys stiffen and stick

WEAK:

the tone has a harder character

STRONG:

the tone hardens

WEAK:

it makes sounds more like something being tortured.

STRONG:

it whines and groans as if tortured.

7. *Replace passive verbs.* Use the active voice. The passive voice fattens on lazy uses of *to be:*

PASSIVE:

Gooden's next pitch was lined by Boggs into left.

ACTIVE:

Boggs lined Gooden's next pitch into left.

PASSIVE:

This bread was baked by Mr. Schiller.

ACTIVE:

Mr. Schiller baked this bread.

PASSIVE:

In the scene it was proved that Gatsby was innocent.

ACTIVE:

The scene proved Gatsby innocent.

As you can see, sometimes one fatty usage leads to another—in this case, a sagging *it* developed a passive verb, which led to a lazy *was*.

One warning about all this butchering. You can't always cut out an *is,* or a *which,* or a *there.* These words have their uses. "It is hot," for example—two empty calories out of three—can't really be tightened or improved. The same is true of the passive voice—a writer will now and then use it purposefully, as Russell Baker does on page 150. When Baker writes, "Kerosene lamps were cleaned and polished," the passive expresses a child's feeling of distance from grown-up chores, as if they somehow get done magically without a *doer.*

Writing isn't a matter of rule, but of taste. Read, write, and ruthlessly edit, and you won't mistake fat for good meat.

CORRECT DOESN'T COUNT

When you trim the fat, you're strengthening, not correcting. No grammar book would complain of "the keys become stiff or sticky." It's correct, but that doesn't make it good. Many people write empty, deceitful prose that is perfectly "correct." But many people don't get in to First Choice University. Think about what you're trying to say and *don't be concerned about correctness.*

Why not? Because admissions officers—not being editors or English teachers—don't know or care much about the fine points of grammar. Most admissions officers—like many writers, and most of the rest of us—wouldn't know which is correct:

    A. Chris is one of those reporters who always meets his deadline.
    B. Chris is one of those reporters who always meet their deadlines.

Even admissions readers who *do* know can't pause long enough to think about it, and it doesn't make much difference. (B is correct; "who" refers to reporters, not Chris.)

I don't mean throw grammar and punctuation out the window. Just don't *think* about it. Unless you have problems with the basics—periods at the end of sentences, subject-verb agreement—it's not an issue. By senior year you know enough grammar to write a college essay. Use what you're familiar with and don't get fancy. Concentrate on the writing.

Spelling is different. I've seen otherwise intelligent admissions officers get themselves into a lather about student spelling, as if it mattered. (Usually because the applicant misspelled the name of the college.)

In the era of spell check, the expectation is that your piece will be perfect. But remember:

Spill chick it goon, bus in it no enough. Pleas hare a fried red you're wort, be case your mite makes man mistook an no seen them wan you rear threw you daft. Think you.

Even so, one typo or spelling error won't sink you as much as an empty idea, vaguely developed.

TAKE THE TIME TO BE SHORT

As you may be beginning to see, it takes time to simplify. If I plan a week in advance to drive to French Lick, Indiana, I will probably consult a map and take the shortest route. But if I must leave *now,* with no time to plot a course, I'll probably get lost or go the long way around. It takes time—and effort—to be quick.

I'm going to start with the assumption that you're a Last-Minute Louie (or Louise). I, too, am one. I know people who prepare for weeks—outlining, sharpening pencils like mad, and stacking up neat piles of paper—and finish days ahead of schedule. They are beneath contempt. But because I am so slow, I know the lengths you have to go to leave yourself enough time at the end to be ruthless in revision. If you know you're a deadline dawdler, set yourself an artificial limit way ahead of your actual schedule: tell a friend or a teacher or whoever's serving as your reader that you'll have a polished final draft ready to read a week before your deadline. This sounds silly and transparent, but it works—you'll usually miss your phony deadline too, but not by much, and then you'll have three or four days to mull over your final draft and buff it to a high sheen.

You must figure into your schedule a time to put your essay away for a day or two when you have finished a complete draft. Getting away from it allows you to come back with fresh eyes. Weaknesses you missed before suddenly cry out, and new ideas arrive for transitions, for endings, for refining the lead. The shape of the whole and the details are visible when you can look at them as if for the first time.

Taking time also helps you be ruthless. The writer of the bathroom essay cut this paragraph, originally the fourth in the piece, entirely:

> I'm not sure I know why it happens, but it works in almost any bathroom, though ones with windows are especially good. I have to admit the bathroom is a strange place for inspiration. Most people don't want to think about the bathroom, something you can tell from the dishonest name we've given it. (I've seen plenty of bathrooms without bathtubs and even showers, but never one without a toilet.) Why not call it the "toiletroom," to be accurate? Or something upbeat

like SaniRama? My little brother calls it "baffroom," a good name. It sounds like a fast-car noise in a cartoon.

It's a good paragraph. It's funny, and it says something. The writer worked hard on it and never thought about doing without it. Then, after putting the essay away, he had two problems: (1) he saw this paragraph as a digression, and (2) the whole essay was too long. So the paragraph had to go.

What is too long? The Common App states only a *minimum* word limit: 250. But the ballpark figure is 500 words. Is 600 too long? No. 700? Not necessarily. But remember your readers. In almost thirty years of teaching I have never—not once—been handed an essay that could not have been cut down and that would not have been better at least a little shorter.

But now let's look at what all this rewriting and editing does for an essay, from notes to final draft.

9

EVOLUTION OF AN ESSAY

One college requests in a supplement, "Please share with us what you believe other students would learn from you, both inside and outside the classroom."

Tough assignment. The temptation to pretend to be something you're not, or to recite your accomplishments, is almost overwhelming. What can you say? "I hope other students will learn from me the values of hard work and fun as well." Ugh. It leads easily to the Jock or the 3D essay. One young woman a number of years ago, knowing the traps buried in the assignment, began by leafing through her notebook. She came across an entry that seems quaint to us today, though its idea and spirit are very contemporary:

My sister is a kick. Seven years old, and she's the only one who knows how to run the VCR. So now she wants one of her own for Christmas. Whatever happened to AM-FM radio for kids? At her age I thought fiddling around with the wires to get a clear picture on *The Brady Bunch* was pretty good. Mom is out of it, can't even deal with cable, can't get her radio to work without static. Sister's already working on computers in school. I feel bad for Mom—some of the stuff even I can't figure out. New technology is fine, I guess, given the fact that

I like old movies on the VCR too, but there has to be something else. What? I don't know. Bike trips?

Using this as a starting point, she wrote a draft:

When I asked my seven-year-old sister what she wanted for Christmas last year, her answer was short, simple and automatic. "Uh . . . Get-In-Shape-Girls, My Little Pony and a VCR."

I can remember the days (and hey—that's not so long ago) when it was crazy for kids to want even a cassette recorder. AM-FM radio was about as far as any of us got. As for television, I used to think I was a big shot because I knew just which wire to twist to erase the fuzzy-static sound that was forever drowning out the entire Brady Bunch. But now my seven-year-old sister is the one who teaches the rest of us about the latest technology. She is official keeper of the VCR. That's because she's the only one who *really* knows how to make it do all the things it's designed to. Mom, meanwhile, still can't tune in her favorite radio station on our Casio Supreme Stereo, and she's helpless when faced with the mesmerizing, ominous "Cable Box." A few months ago I watched my sister try to show Mom which buttons to push to record a TV show that would be on later that day. The generation gap is getting wider in our house, byte by byte, chip by chip.

So one of the things my future classmates will not be learning from me is how to adjust to changes in home entertainment. They'll have to see my sister for that. I'm just too old to understand.

I've also learned a few other things from my sister. Last summer we flew from New York to London in only six hours, which didn't make much of an impression on my sister. She didn't understand why it took so *long.* From my point of view, the ride was a far cry from spectacular; the cabin was cramped, the wallpaper and seat coverings were dizzying, the air was clogged by the stench of old sneakers and formaldehyde, the food (?) was disgusting, and somewhere along the line I lost five hours of my life. Where that time went I'll never understand, but at least it had the decency to come back four weeks later, upon my return home.

When she had gotten this far, the writer stopped to ask, Where am I? She originally wanted to say she hoped other students might learn from her how much fun bike trips and the outdoors could be, as opposed to the kind of prepackaged entertainment she saw around her all the time. Anyway, she knew she had nothing against the VCR—she liked it in fact. But in avoiding the dumb sounding "I hope people learn from me that bike trips are fun," she had gotten off the track, writing about her sister and their different attitudes. She was not getting very quickly to what other students would learn from her in college. Where did this airplane business lead? She could start revising sections now—that would be one way to try to pick up the thread of the main idea—but it was too soon for that. Since she was rolling along toward her bike story, she decided to get it out and see where it led:

I have also ridden a bicycle across Canada, 750 miles in 28 days, during which time it rained for two weeks straight. Needless to say, I learned to appreciate the sun. As it happens, I also learned to enjoy the rain. My journey was slow, yes. But it was refreshing (there is a small brook in Algonquin Park with water so cold it could chill a penguin), informative (an old man in Whitney Ontario will tell you more about trout fishing than you'll ever want to know), and far more beautiful (from the soft evergreens lining Fodder Pond to the hard cobblestone streets in Old Quebec) than any voyage through darkness in an oblong metal box could ever hope to be.

I am no naturalist; I don't eat bark. I like junk food as much as the next person, and I am the first to run to the video shop when my family wants a movie for that VCR. But I have discovered along the way that one thing does not have to exclude the other. I can only teach people that which I myself have already learned. And I would take pride in showing someone first hand that popcorn tastes just as good while you're watching a sunset from a mountaintop as it does while you're watching an old movie.

This draft has many merits. The writer has observed carefully and much of the writing is alive. But it's not coherent—it's like two different essays, one about TV and VCRs and technology, the other about learning and teaching and her family. But she knew she didn't have time for two different essays. She tried to find ways to connect them, or cut one out, which meant thinking about the lead and the end, and what the connection might be. She was thinking of shape.

The end seemed fine for the time being. But the lead, even though it was anecdotal, didn't lead anywhere. She cut the original opening and tried a few new ones:

> I used to think I was a big shot because I knew just which wire to twist to erase the fuzzy-static sound that was forever drowning out the entire Brady Bunch.

Or:

> There are a few things my classmates *won't* learn from me.

She thought the last one was good because it got into the teaching and learning idea—the point of the assignment, after all—quickly. A little negative, though. She hunted in her ending for another lead that might do the trick differently: "I can only teach that which I myself have already learned." And seeing this line, she couldn't help improving it: "I can only teach what I have already learned."

Then, thinking of her sister again, she added: ". . . which seems to be shrinking compared to what everyone else knows."

She tried keeping the learning idea but starting with her sister:

> In my life I have many teachers and a mother who likes to lecture, but it's my sister, age seven, who does most of the teaching.

Working on the lead made her start to understand what her essay might be about. And thinking of her sister at the beginning made her think of the ending, and how far away she had gotten from her sister. She liked writing about her sister and thought it would be good to shape the essay around her, if possible. But how to get back to her? The writer changed the last line to:

> And I would take pride in showing someone (maybe even my sister when she's old enough) first hand that popcorn tastes just as good while you're watching a sunset from a mountaintop as it does while you're watching an old movie.

Something good was beginning to happen. But she also worried about the middle of the essay. The travel stories wandered. Could she find something in the beginning and the end that might bind the middle? Young sister, the writer feeling so old by comparison, technology, movies, popcorn, teaching and learning?

Seeing the vague "other things" in the first sentence of the airplane paragraph, she changed it to:

> I've also learned how to take other technology for granted from my sister.

And at the end of that paragraph, picking up on the time idea:

> I wondered if I kept flying east, would I get younger and younger (and
> eventually understand things)?

That was a funny idea—that people might actually know less and less as
they approached twenty-one. It wasn't serious, of course, but it might be a
good connection to what her sister and maybe her classmates could learn
from her—an idea she was already trying to bring out at the end.

Then she thought of beginning the next-to-last paragraph with this:

> Without my sister, I have also ridden . . .

Which quickly developed into:

> There are a few things I haven't been too old to learn on my own,
> though. While my sister went to camp, I rode a bicycle . . .

Where was all this going? Did she have a main idea? She tried stating
it: "Someone might learn from me that there are things worth more than
the latest gadget." But it wasn't that bike trips were *worth* more than VCRs.
Maybe, "Someone might learn from me about pleasures at least as satisfy-
ing as the latest gadget." Or something like that. She'd come back to it.

Now, with her destination getting clearer, she hoped honing some
sentences would make the whole idea sharper in her mind. Already she
had changed "fuzzy static sound" to "static." She substituted the single,
exact "alien" for the two words "mesmerizing, ominous," as well as "widening" for "getting wider." (Weak use of "get"; remember?) She deleted
"that would be on later that day" as unnecessary. She also changed "upon
my return" (too formal) to "when we flew home," and "during which
time" to "when." If it really was "needless to say," she didn't need to say

it, and "as it happens" was just conversational filler; the piece did not lose
its friendly tone without them. The stench "of" old sneakers and formaldehyde was wrong. (Although a few old sneakers might have found their
way on board, formaldehyde probably hadn't.) She changed "of" to "like,"
creating the simile she had intended in the first place.

Here's the first rewrite. (She added the brackets around trouble spots
afterward.)

Though I have many teachers and a mom who likes to lecture, in my
life it's my sister, age seven, who does most of the instructing. After
all, she's the only one who really knows how to make the VCR do
everything it's designed to. I used to think I was a big shot when I was
her age because I knew just which wire to twist to erase the fuzzy-
static [that was forever drowning out] the Brady Bunch. My mom still
can't tune in her favorite radio station on our Casio Supreme Stereo,
and she's helpless when faced with the alien cable box. A few months
ago I watched my sister try to show her which buttons to push to record a TV show. Poor Mom—the generation gap is widening in our
house, byte by byte, chip by chip.

I've also learned to take other technology for granted from my
sister. Last summer we flew from New York to London in only six
hours, [which] didn't impress her much. She didn't understand why
it took so *long*. (There's nothing more jaded than a seven-year-old.)
[From my point of view], the ride was [a far cry] from spectacular; the
cabin was cramped, the wallpaper and seat coverings were dizzying,
the air was clogged by a stench like old sneakers and formaldehyde,
the food (?) was disgusting, and [somewhere along the line] I lost five
hours of my life. Where that time went I'll never understand, but at
least it had the decency to come back four weeks later when we flew
home. What would have happened if I kept flying east? Would I get
younger and younger (and eventually understand things)?

[There are] a few [things] I haven't been too old to learn on my own, though. While my sister went to camp, I rode a bicycle across Canada, 750 miles in 28 days, when it rained for two weeks straight. I learned to appreciate the sun, but I also learned to enjoy the rain. My journey was slow, yes. But it was refreshing ([there is] a small brook in Algonquin Park with water so cold it could chill a penguin) informative (an old man in Whitney Ontario [will tell you] more about trout fishing than [you'll ever want to know]), and far more beautiful (from the soft evergreens lining Fodder Pond to the hard cobblestone streets in Old Quebec) than any voyage through darkness in an oblong metal box [could ever hope to be.]

I am no naturalist; I don't eat bark. I like junk food as much as the next person, and I am the first to run to the video shop when my family wants a movie for that VCR. But I have discovered [along the way] that one [thing] does not have to exclude the other. I can only teach people what I have already learned. And I would take pride in showing someone (maybe even my sister when she's old enough) first hand that popcorn tastes just as good while you're watching a sunset from a mountaintop as it does while you're watching an old movie.

At this point, the lead still wasn't right, and she didn't have the solution to the problem of the end. She decided now was a good time to put it away for a while.

Two days later, looking at it fresh, she rewrote the lead and the last paragraph where most of the trouble was, three more times, grinding slowly to get the ideas right. The end had to tie it all together, and it didn't yet.

She didn't really like the assignment very much, and she wanted the ending to reflect the honest humility she felt about it. In the beginning she had tried, in a light way, to say that she didn't like to teach. She liked learning from example, and from doing things. So she decided to change "take pride in showing someone," because it sounded so teachy. It took most of a Saturday afternoon to finish.

I think my classmates might learn more from my sister. She's seven. I'm not much of a teacher, and neither is my mom, though like a lot of moms she likes to lecture. But around here my sister, who doesn't even know how to lecture, does most of the instructing. After all, she's the only one who really can make the VCR do everything it's designed to. I used to think I was a big shot when I was her age because I knew just which wire to twist to erase the static drowning out *The Brady Bunch*. Mom is even worse than I am—she still can't tune in her favorite radio station on our Casio Supreme, and she's helpless when faced with the alien cable box, never mind the VCR. A few months ago I watched my sister try to show her which buttons to push to record a TV show. Poor Mom—the generation gap is widening in our house, byte by byte, chip by chip.

My sister has also taught me how to take other inventions in stride. Last summer we flew from New York to London in only six hours. My sister wasn't impressed. She didn't understand why it took so *long*. (There's nothing more jaded than a seven-year-old.) I tried to be blasé too, but it wasn't easy. The cabin was cramped, the wallpaper and seat coverings were dizzying, the air was clogged by a stench like old sneakers and formaldehyde, the food was disgusting, and I lost five hours of my life. Where that time went I'll never understand, but at least it had the decency to come back four weeks later when we flew home. What would have happened if I kept flying east? Would I get younger and younger (and eventually be seven and finally Understand Things)?

There are a few lessons I haven't been too old to learn on my own, though. While my sister went to camp that same summer, I rode a bicycle across Canada with ten other people, 750 miles in twenty-eight days. It rained for two weeks straight. Needless to say, I learned to appreciate the sun. I also learned to enjoy the rain. My journey was slow but refreshing (a small brook in Algonquin Park runs so cold it could chill a penguin), informative (an old man in Whitney, Ontario, told me more about trout fishing than I can remember), and far more beautiful (from the soft evergreens lining Fodder Pond to the hard cobblestone streets in Old Quebec) than any high speed voyage through darkness in an oblong metal box.

But I'm no bark-munching naturalist. In fact, I eat as much popcorn as the next person, who happens to be my sister, the popcorn queen. And I'm always feeding that same VCR an old movie to have with my popcorn. I live in both these worlds, my sister's up-to-the-minute New York and the slower satisfactions of bike trips through the country. I don't know if anyone could learn something from that combination, though it's pretty important to me. But someone—maybe even my sister, when she's no longer young enough to know everything—might find out from me first hand that popcorn tastes just as good while you're watching a sunset from a mountaintop as it does while you're watching *Gone With the Wind*. Maybe even better.

It's impossible to show every change, every rejected phrase—that would require another whole book—but I hope you get an idea of the distance an essay must travel before it's ready to make the final trip to the admissions office.

Next I want to suggest a few ways to stretch one essay idea across many of the sometimes bizarre questions colleges ask.

READING

10

A NOT-BRIEF-ENOUGH RANT ABOUT SUPPLEMENTS

(or, Will Someone Please Scrap the Common App?)

S upplement.

Sounds as nourishing and as easy to take as chewable orange vitamin C or a chocolate protein smoothie, doesn't it?

Yuh, right.

The Common Application was originally intended to streamline and organize the process of applying for college, but its wide adoption by so many schools has created exactly the opposite effect. Many colleges, for obscure reasons of their own, now require the Common App *and* a litter of their own supplements.

Are we having fun yet?

The creature called *The Supplement*, in fact, has swelled in the competitive admissions environment like a sci-fi reptile in an overheated lagoon. So now you'll sometimes write *more* than students who applied in the BCA (Before Common App) era, when every school had its own application and you could finagle and adapt a way to write, maybe, two essays. You were born too late.

Colleges with extensive supplements (are you listening, Yale, Harvard, Penn, Chicago, et al.?) would be more honest *and* make it less of a pain for students if they just abandoned the Common App and went back to their individual applications. They're already doing it anyway.

MIT and Georgetown, which do not accept the Common App, are humanely leading the way. Dartmouth, to its credit, makes do with only the Common App essay. That's the other sensible way to go.

Call me an oversimplifier, but I don't get why, in the Internet age, each school doesn't just create its own online application. All students have access to computers, at least at school or public libraries, even at the most underfunded ones. No printing and paper costs. I'm already writing all my recommendations online at the Naviance site, and most colleges are now completely paperless in their file reading.

But enough rant. How to make the practical best of this?

Certain truths endure. Essay topics come in two basic types: Generals and Specials. A General is broad and open-ended. *Discuss an experience or influence*, for example. A Special is narrow, like *Find x*, or *Write an essay somehow inspired by super-huge mustard*. (Those were recent University of Chicago topics.) All the Common App topics (see below) are Generals. Supplements are now almost all Specials.

Supplements also come in two sizes: standard (between 300–500 words), and short takes. But all of them, Specials and Generals of any length, are asking for a *personal statement*. Just as on the Common App, you *always* want to write something vivid, detailed, specific, close to what you know.

The main problem (only a little more rant, I promise) is that after you've written a Common App General, you can't use it or any adaptation of it for *any* supplement, whether General or Special, standard or short.

Still, the goal is to try to limit your Generals and write the fewest possible Specials.

Every school asks: Why do you want to go to First Choice?

I know I want to learn to write well. When my college adviser told me about First Choice, I was happy to see on the website "a national leader in teaching students to write effectively, learn from each other, and think for themselves." I also know I want to study history, so I browsed through the course catalog. It was as if someone had based a whole department just on my interests. I was amazed by the volume and diversity of the professors' research: medieval religious dissent, the modern Mexican military, mountaineering, the Stalinist campaign against Islam, nineteenth-century German working-class autobiographies. In the classes I attended the professors were incredibly knowledgeable and the students engaged. The campus seemed to be teeming with excitement and enthusiasm, and my tour guide was one of the most charming people I have ever met. The community seemed completely at ease and happy to be there. I immediately felt welcomed. The college seems designed to create this comfortable environment, with clusters of couches and chairs in Oz Hall and the rooms in the student center dedicated to group study. I really like the idea that students are encouraged to engage each other. My college adviser said there is a floor of the library dedicated entirely to history. I can easily imagine myself spending a lot of time in there.

This 200–plus word response is straightforward and clear. It could be more specific about the campus atmosphere—one detail or incident would have helped—but it's based on a specific personal response. The rest of the application will have to back up the history passion, but the voice is unpretentious (almost chatty) though the subject is the academic atmosphere. Be careful your piece doesn't sound like a generic form paragraph with downloaded plugged-in factoids.

If you had cut the above to 100 words (about 500 characters), it might look like this:

I am happy to see on the website "a national leader in teaching students to write effectively, learn from each other, and think for themselves." The history courses look as if someone had based a curriculum on my interests: medieval religious dissent, the modern Mexican military, Stalin and Islam. On my visit the students were engaged and happy to be there. The college seems designed to create this comfortable environment, with clusters of couches and chairs and rooms dedicated to group study. An entire library floor is dedicated to history. I imagine myself spending a lot of time there.

There's no getting around writing one of these for every school that asks. It's true of engineering schools, too, which often have a very specific "why engineering?" topic. Detail is still the key. You can imagine the generic clichés: "First Choice has a world-renowned faculty and top students and facilities, and I feel confident I could reach my true potential there." Blagh. Better: "I haven't visited yet, but my friend Deirdre, who's a sophomore there, says her brilliant environmental engineering professor has just discovered how to make limitless energy out of sewage, and she's already arranged a summer internship through one of her other professors." If you can't write *something* specific and personal—if you're applying only because the college "has a name," you need to do some research and examine why, in fact, you *are* applying. And be careful about your sources; on the website, every place looks remarkably similar: a multicultural paradise of youthful intellectual bliss complete with brick buildings, bicycles, and a body of water.

TO OPT OR NOT TO OPT

Are "optional" essays truly optional? Tufts, Duke, and others, with an almost hopeless sense of defeat because they know you won't believe them, insist mightily they are. (The colleges doth protest too much, methinks.

If they don't need them, why provide a topic? Why suggest anything at all, if their strenuous denial shows they know full well applicants will interpret the slightest suggestion through the screen of anxiety? I'm just asking.) In the current market, one of the things colleges try to gauge is the authenticity and depth of an applicant's interest. Have you been to campus, did you attend the session at your high school when an admission officer visited? One way to show interest is to respond to the optional essays.

Let's look at how to write one piece that satisfies a welter of supplement Specials, optional or not.

Let's suppose among your applications are Chicago, Princeton, Brown, Penn, and Johns Hopkins. (Though there'll be, let's say, four more, not every school wants a new standard-length essay.)

No human being can write all these essays while also passing senior year. So you need to find a way to consolidate, to use one piece for all these.

First line up the required supplement choices:

Princeton (Pick one; 500 words)

- Tell us about a person who has influenced you in a significant way.
- Using the statement below as a starting point, tell us about an event or experience that helped you define one of your values or changed how you approach the world.

  "Princeton in the Nation's Service" was the title of a speech given by Woodrow Wilson on the 150th anniversary of the University. It became the unofficial Princeton motto and was expanded for the University's 250th anniversary to "Princeton in the nation's service and in the service of all nations."—Woodrow Wilson, Princeton Class of 1879, served on the faculty and was Princeton's president from 1902–1910.

- Using the following quotation from "The Moral Obligations of Living in a Democratic Society" as a starting point, tell us about an event or experience that helped you define one of your values or changed how you approach the world.

"Empathy is not simply a matter of trying to imagine what others are going through, but having the will to muster enough courage to do something about it. In a way, empathy is predicated upon hope."—Cornel West, Class of 1943, University Professor in the Center for African American Studies, Princeton University.

- Using a favorite quotation from an essay or book you have read in the last three years as a starting point, tell us an event or experience that helped you define one of your values or changed how you approach the world. Please write the quotation at the beginning of your essay.

Brown (Pick one; 300 words or fewer)

A. Why are you going to college?

B. Sculptor Jacques Lipchitz once said, "Cubism is like standing at a certain point on a mountain and looking around. If you go higher, things will look different; if you go lower, again they will look different. It is a point of view." With this in mind, describe a moment when your perspective changed.

C. What question could we ask to gain the most insight into you? What is your answer?

Chicago (Pick one; a "one- or two-page response")

1. "What does Play-Doh™ have to do with Plato?"—*The 2011 University of Chicago Scavenger Hunt List*

     Every May, the University of Chicago hosts the world's largest scavenger hunt. As part of this year's hunt, students raced to find the shortest path between two seemingly unrelated things by traveling through Wikipedia articles.

     Wikipedia is so passé. Without the help of everyone's favorite collaborative internet encyclopedia, show us your own unique path from Play-Doh™ to Plato.

2. Observation, Hypothesis, Experiment, Analysis, Conclusion; since the 17th century, the scientific method has been the generally accepted way to investigate, explore, and acquire new knowledge. The actual process of intellectual discovery, however, is rarely so simple or objective. The human mind often leaps from observation to conclusion with ease, rushes headlong into hypothesis-less experiments, or dwells on the analysis, refusing to conclude.

     Tell us about your non-scientific method. (Diagrams, graphs, and/or visual aids allowed within your essay.)

3. Spanish poet Antonio Machado wrote, "Between living and dreaming there is a third thing. Guess it." Give us your guess.

4. While working at the Raytheon Company, Percy Spencer noticed that standing in front of a magnetron (used to generate microwave radio signals) caused a chocolate bar in his pocket to melt. He then placed a bowl of corn in front of the device, and soon it was popping all over the room. A couple of years later, Raytheon was selling the first commercial microwave oven.

     Write about a time you found something you weren't looking for.

5. In the spirit of adventurous inquiry, pose a question of your own. If your prompt is original and thoughtful, then you should have little trouble writing a great essay. Draw on your best qualities as a writer, thinker, visionary, social critic, sage, citizen of the world, or future citizen of the University of Chicago; take a little risk, and have fun.

6. Don't write about reverse psychology.

University of Pennsylvania (approximately 500 words)

Considering both the specific undergraduate school or program to which you are applying and the broader University of Pennsylvania community, what academic, research, and/or extracurricular paths do you see yourself exploring at Penn?

Johns Hopkins (250 word maximum each)

1. Johns Hopkins offers 50 majors across the schools of Arts & Sciences and Engineering. On this application, we ask you to identify one or two that you might like to pursue here. Why did you choose the way you did? If you are undecided, why didn't you choose? (If any past courses or academic experiences influenced your decision, you may include them in your essay.)

2. Tell us something about yourself or your interests that we wouldn't learn by looking at the rest of your application materials. (While you should still pay attention to sentence structure and grammar, your response is meant as a way for us to get to know you, rather than a formal essay.)

I know—incredibly annoying and difficult, despite the creative efforts of Chicago, for example. (Chicago, one of the nation's great intellectual force fields, is combatting its image as a place, according to T-shirts sold and worn all over its own campus, "where fun goes to die.") Plus there's the length issue. Start with a 500–word piece, then cut it down.

It's going to contain a quotation that poses a question (Princeton), or that you pose a question about (Chicago and Brown), that tells something about your academic or extracurricular interests they wouldn't know from the application (Hopkins and Penn).

A few possible beginnings might look something like these:

• "Cauliflower is nothing but a cabbage with a college education," said Mark Twain in *Pudd'nhead Wilson*. The question is, did the cabbage want to become a cauliflower, and if so, how did it use four years of college to do it? I haven't read every page of your course catalog, so I don't know if you even offer Cauliflowering as a major. At this point I certainly count myself among the cabbages, and I certainly have no idea what I want to specialize in. But I do know this: I am looking forward in college to transformation if not flowering. . . .

- If the goal of a college education is a search for truth, what am I supposed to make of Nobel Prize–winning playwright Harold Pinter, who said, "A thing is not necessarily true or false; it can be both true and false"? Is his own statement both true and false? What would that mean? This is the kind of question my friend Avital and I like to ask, and the kind of thing I expect to use my four years to explore.

- I'm left-handed. I'm also a Red Sox fan. These are not credentials many colleges appear to be interested in, but I have always taken some comfort from a Boston southpaw and guru from the 1980s named Bill Lee, whose quotation has been taped to my wall since I was nine: "You have two hemispheres in your brain—a left and a right side. The left side controls the right side of your body and right controls the left half. It's a fact. Therefore, left-handers are the only people in their right minds." In my right mind I also have an interest in science I don't yet know what to do with, though I know that "handedness" has become interesting to neurologists, as it is to me. But it's the lefty choices and stereotypes that I also would like to pursue . . .

The important thing here is to find a quotation that not only stimulates you but also comes from a personally meaningful source and not just a few minutes' random googling for something that "sounds good," the Robert-Frost-road-less-traveled cliché.

This connect-the-dots method is actually helpful, because it sets up limitations that can focus your ideas and make the game worth playing, like the net in tennis. Incidentally, after writing one of these for the schools that require it, you now have a piece you can often use as-is for other required or "optionals" as well:

Describe your intellectual interests, their evolution, and what makes them exciting to you. [Cornell]

1. Reflect on an idea or experience important to your intellectual development. 2. Write a note to your future roommate that reveals something about you or that will help your roommate and us know you better. 3. What matters to you and why. [Stanford, all three required, at least 250 words each, but not exceeding space provided.]

Describe what you expect your academic journey at Bowdoin to include.

Tell us something that you would like us to know about you that we might not get from the rest of your application—or something that you would like a chance to say more about. [Yale, required, fewer than 500 words]

Why did you do it? [Tufts, optional, 250–500 words]

Describe the environment in which you were raised—your family, home, neighborhood or community—and how it influenced the person you are today. [Tufts, required, 200–250 words]

Use the richness of your identity to frame your personal outlook. [Tufts, required, 200–250 words]

What intrigues you? [NYU, about 300 words]

Amherst requires you to "respond" to one of a handful of quotations in "no more than 300 words."

11

EXHIBITS: THE QUICK
AND THE DULL

Here are a few student essays to help sharpen your judgment. As you read each one, ask yourself what you learn about the writer, and whether you like the person you see.

I have asked a small group of current and former admissions officers—Lifers and Temps from a few of the nation's most selective colleges—to respond to them exactly as they would in reading applications. They saw only what you see below, the essays themselves—no other parts of the applications. Evaluating the essays out of their usual context is tricky, but in most cases it didn't seem to bother my panelists; what you hear from them is a good sampling of backstage admissions talk. In order to allow them to speak so freely, they are identified only by number after each essay. In some cases I've added a postscript to clarify their readings.

Remember that this is only a sampling. Like many other admissions officers, my panelists have strong opinions that are sometimes unreasonable. For instance, many admissions officers dislike essays about the application process itself, which they feel shows an unappealing "sweatiness." In other words, colleges are glad to be extremely selective, but they don't like it when you are aware of that. They want you to act as if pressure, or even the application itself, doesn't exist, and that the whole process is simply a nice chat between you and them.

You may also notice that they love to play amateur psychologist. It's an occupational hazard.

But the most important lesson here is seeing how often admissions people disagree. Different readers, even in the same admissions office, look for different things. I remember epic battles with admissions colleagues over whether an essay showed a student was a potential scholar or just a nerd, a future physicist or just a pre-med. How can you please them? You can't. Say what *you* have to say. The exact same essay, placed in the files of two different students with comparable academic credentials, might lead to different results. Essay (E) didn't prevent the writer, a Just Folks applicant, from being admitted to one of the two or three most selective colleges in the country, despite the outrage of my panelists. This chapter, above all, will show how senseless it is to ask, "What are they looking for?" They—as a group, as a college—don't always know themselves.

(A) Describe the greatest challenge you have faced or expect to face.

Except for my struggle with jacks—I could never get past sixies while Leslie Ackerman whizzed through tenzies and back to onezies all in one turn—this application is the greatest challenge I've faced. I'm glad you didn't ask how I dealt with it.

I hope I'm not dodging or taking the easy way out. It's hard to find an honest answer to your question. Nothing I've done so far could be called a "great challenge." A minor annoyance, maybe: there was my brush with Physics, when I tried to understand the practical results of impractical problems, like where an iron ball will land if thrown out of a moving car. (When I brought up in class that I never *would* throw an iron ball out of a moving car, Mr. Weitz just looked at me.) Before that came the separate trials of learning the Australian crawl and the slice backhand, the first for water survival and the second, my parents said, for social survival. And, of course, the intensely competitive jacks. (At age nine, to be the best jacks player was also to be the most popular girl.) All these experiences were difficult—getting anything right in tennis still seems more like a miracle—but I can't imagine calling one of them my "greatest challenge."

Challenge seems like it should be something bigger, and I'm not sure I've faced it yet. I've never had to work to support my family, as my mother did when she was my age. Unlike my older brother, I've never had to find an affordable apartment in New York City. I've never even experienced what some of my New Jersey friends say is the greatest challenge of all—fighting the 8:00 A.M. traffic on the George Washington Bridge, unsure if they'll ever get to school. I live in Manhattan, which, now that I think about it, may be challenge enough for anyone. But that's probably not what you had in mind.

Putting together these forms for you, on the other hand, comes closer to what I think of as "challenge." That may be only because I want to go to Dartmouth more than I ever wanted to imitate Chris Evert Lloyd. But part of the challenge has to do with what applying to college means—writing essays, remembering teachers and classes and sports, answering questions, all this self examination. At least in physics problems there was always a formula to plug in. But there are no "correct" answers, everybody keeps telling me, on the application; there's not even a correct method, where you can get points for reaching the wrong answer the right way. There's only me. It's a serious challenge, if not a great one, to distill on four sides of blue paper the person I've become in seventeen years. It's like trying to put myself into a little jar—a jar of Justine—and yet somehow hoping that I won't fit, that I can't be categorized. The whole thing makes sevenzies look easy.

1. I usually dislike essays about how hard the process is (which is what they must get nine out of ten times in response to this question), but at least this has a warm, funny tone to it that's appealing. Don't learn much about the kid, though.

2. (This is a *dumb* question—part of the reason her answer is so weak. She's never faced, at seventeen or eighteen, a real challenge. If she has faced one, she hasn't got enough perspective to know it.) However—to her response: Useless! I have no interest in her anxiety about the college process. All I learn from this is that she'd be overcome if she ever faced a *significant* challenge.

3. Too pat and attempts to be cute and humorous. Much of the essay seems addressed to the admissions committee in an overly self-conscious way. The clever trick doesn't work here.

4. Breezy, savvy, lighthearted but well-written essay.

Sometimes you have to put up with a college's essay assignment. Although she wrote about applying—a no-no, usually—the result is a good piece. Two admissions officers for, two against.

(B) Describe a person who has influenced you.

I have always wanted to take his picture there in rehearsal, when he stands in the middle of a semicircle of upturned eyes and open mouths, grandiosely waving his endless arms as though he were swimming through the music. At eight-thirty in the morning, when the rest of us are barely awake, Conrad Burkhalter is at his lovable best. The sun opposite me shines on the sopranos and altos and silhouettes his aristocratic nose, shaggy brows and frizz of hair against the window pane and the morning sky.

"Rrrroll your R's!" he says. Then he stomps and wiggles, bellows and whispers, puts his fingers to his chin as if in prayer and opens his blue eyes so wide they seem to leap out directly into mine, to discover that mine are closed; I am nodding asleep to the march rhythms of Haydn's *Mass in Time of War*. But not for long. He goes through every conceivable contortion and exertion to energize our eighty sleepy faces. It is as if his wild gestures could conduct electricity as well as music through the drowsy air into our voices. Sometimes I wonder what he would do if we returned in kind, bugging our eyes out, wriggling and twisting our bodies to the music. As it is, we continue to hold our notes too long or not long enough and we refuse to "dance" with the 3/4 time.

Every once in a while he launches into a boiling tirade—he "Swisses out." Then he reverts to European discipline: "If not every person is in this room at exactly eighteen minutes past eight o'clock, there will be no concert." He is the quintessential Swiss in other ways as well: we must learn to speak English, not Americanese, we must not be "cool" when singing Haydn, we must get eight hours of sleep, be prompt, attentive, enunciate our consonants, and think about nothing else. This is the law according to Burkhalter.

It works. His ridiculous energy and steaming rages do make us sit straighter, hold our scores higher and try a little harder. When he pleads, "Both feet on the floor—you cannot hope to sing if you do not support yourself," there is a second or two of shuffling and creaking as 160 legs are uncrossed. Then he spreads his own feet wide and arches his back a little, sticking out his pot belly and hitching up his belt. He's forever tucking in a stubborn shirt tail set free by quick tempi or forte passages. There is a lot of child in him. He can glower as furiously as a two-year-old when he says "Elephants have memories, people have pencils—write it down!" or he can smile so widely and coyly that I am afraid his grin will devour his ears and like Beethoven he will have to conduct from memory.

Of all my teachers, I feel the most loyalty to him because he devotes his entire self to his work. He does more than just wheedle a

Haydn Mass out of us at a sleepy hour; his endless arm is as ready to wrap itself around my shoulder with a reassuring squeeze as it is to gyrate in 4/4 time, and he gives advice and drops of Burk-wisdom as freely as musical instruction. When he sits behind his messy desk after rehearsal and we sprawl—legs, arms, chatter, bookbags—on the couch in his comfortable office, he looks like a complacent Swiss Buddha, nodding and smiling those blue eyes at us, always there, always quirky, always inspiring to me.

1. Send it to *The New Yorker!* A more wonderful piece of description I've never read. The use of language and ability to convey mood is really remarkable. I'd love to have a kid who can write like this in the class.
2. Wonderful. I am the 81st choir member here. I am transported to Burkhalter's rehearsal.
3. Excellent. I like the humor and descriptive quality of this essay. Good, strong, crisp writing.
4. Delightful and affectionate portrayal of choir director who inspires with his energy and commitment. Nice, warm piece.

(C) Tell us anything you think we should know.

The aspect of college I'm anticipating most is the chance to continue to refine my interpersonal skills. In high school I feel I have dedicated myself to academics and extracurriculars, but more especially I have enjoyed the contact with my peers in more informal settings such as the cafeteria or the moments between classes, when friends and acquaintances gather to talk about many subjects and ease the tensions of the school day. And yet high school is somewhat confining in this regard, as a result of spending so much scheduled time in class and, in my case, in being transported to and from school for over an hour each day.

And yet working with people is often the key to success, as I have learned from the computer consulting company I formed with some friends last year. Of course we had to begin with a thorough knowledge of the subject, but the company taught us not only how to run a small business but also how to deal effectively with people—for instance, how to give customers information which is relevant to their questions. We also tutor both children and adults in using their computers, and I think that we have gained some helpful insights into teaching. I have learned that communication is just as important as knowledge, for, without the latter, the former is useless.

My work as assistant editor of the newspaper, a weekly that has won several awards for excellence from the Columbia Scholastic Press, also taught me the value of the personal touch. A good interview, for instance, demands revealing quotations from the subject. In interviewing people it is important to put them at ease before delving into their innermost feelings and ultimately obtaining valuable quotes; many stories unfortunately fall flat because the interviewer has not allowed his subject to relax. I have taken pride in my ability to get people to open up, resulting in a series of interviews that many have found revealing and readable.

In all my endeavors, I have discovered that knowing how to interact with many different varieties of people is invaluable. College, with its diverse social settings, its wide array of people, promises to provide the broad experience that gives education its special flavor. Having roommates from Ohio and Colorado and India can teach as much—maybe more!—than the best textbook or teacher. Although, through my interests in psychology, I plan to benefit academically from whatever college I attend, I am just as eager to benefit from the people I will meet in the course of four years.

1. I could have stopped after the first sentence. (After all, a good pickpocket has, in a sense, "refined his interpersonal skills.") Anyway, we learn a couple of things about the writer, but the statement is poorly written and a dime a dozen.

2. I was getting interested in the computer company job, and then the gears switched. Too bad, because the momentum fizzled out, and is nothing by the end.

3. A walking cliché of an essay with bad grammar to boot. One almost gets ill.

4. Awkward, somewhat disjointed essay.

(D) Any topic.

ONLY AT NIGHT

The above is the title of a story I may someday write. Sordid romance? Spy mystery? Drug novel? Actually, it is a description of my work habits. To the horror of my parents, who are convinced they have brought up some kind of lunatic, I can concentrate only when the house is all mine. At three a.m., I rule the night.

Well, sort of. Unfortunately I cannot boast that I am someone well-adjusted to the night. My mother keeps a tally of the number of times she has opened my bedroom door to find me sprawled on the floor unconscious, buried in blue ink and American history. My appearance-conscious sister has often lectured me on the damaging social effects of dark circles under the eyes. Classes, which have a bad habit of taking place during the day, are often a blur. I don't wait for darkness because *Moby-Dick* or trigonometric functions are any easier by night than by day; it's just that my work seems important, even vital, when I spend precious early morning hours doing it. My father thinks it is the result of too many suspense novels, but I don't know. If sneaking through the house for a bowl of Rice Krispies to keep me awake is the nearest I can come to fulfilling my fantasies of adventure and heroism, Robert Ludlum couldn't have had much of an effect.

Actually, adventure, if not heroism, has not always been that hard to come by. When I was six I would lie open-eyed in bed, waiting with terrified eagerness for a robber's creeping footsteps. I imagined myself bravely rescuing the entire family—that is, until one real creak from an upstairs floorboard would send me scurrying to my parents. But as I've grown older and my nocturnal vigils longer, my hopes of one day gaining the courage I would need in such a situation have only grown dimmer. I remember two exploits especially, one a midnight tramp through the jungles of Central Park with two friends who were searching for an obscure war monument; the other was a panicked call to the police to report a bomb I had seen smoking in the gateway of a sidestreet near my house. (It turned out to be a firecracker.) The park I survived by envisioning myself an undercover archeologist; the "bomb"—a daytime event—is now just a blur of tears and shaking.

The truth is I'm not really suited for night or day, but, responsibilities being what they are, you have to choose one. Though I've put a dent in my habit of classroom dozing with a strong brand of drip coffee, I still really work only in the dark hours of the morning, surrounded by my private goblins. Each to his own muse.

1. Give this person a single room. Humorous in spots and not a bad effort, I guess. But the second half falls off and though likable, he or she'd better have lots else going for him.

2. Be careful with roommate selection.

3. Not bad writing. Above average, but I don't think I got to know the candidate well. Many phrases meant to be clever fell short of their target.

4. Perhaps a bit overdone. Essay is fine but not unusual.

Here are the amateur shrinks. But this statement, with its variation on the Confession lead in the first paragraph, is a good one—notice the admissions officers seem to acknowledge that the writer will get in. (Otherwise there's no need to "be careful with roommate selection.") Their comments tell you how nitpicky they can be. The writer was admitted to one of the most selective colleges in the nation.

(E) Any topic.

NOTES FROM THE UNDERBRED
(WITH HUMBLEST APOLOGIES TO DOSTOEVSKY)

Gentlemen, you probably think I'm applying to your university out of some deep-felt love for the school and that I'll jump up and down and cry if I get rejected. But I assure you that it's all the same to me. Really, gentlemen, I'd be much happier if you rejected me, for nothing would be more horrifying than to spend four years at your despicable institution. I'm joking, of course, and said this merely to shock you. Why, there's actually nothing more appetizing than the idea of spending four years at your holy and venerated institution—I visited there myself, and found the chess-playing facilities to be superb. But in fact, I don't play chess, and the one time I tried I ended up hurling the chessboard at my opponent. It was not the fact that he was constantly practicing psychological subtleties on me—no, his transparent tricks hardly bothered me at all. Rather, it was that this despicable and vain creature—whose name would be known to you gentlemen, if I would only mention it—simply sat there with a beatific smile on his face throughout the game, clasping his hands together and nodding every time I made a move. You laugh, of course, and wonder why that should torment me so. But it was abundantly clear at the time that he felt himself to be superior to me in all respects, not only that of chess, and nothing could have infuriated me more or been further from the truth, for I am actually quite a fine fellow.

Of course, gentlemen, you say to yourself, "I'll be the judge of that!" But in reality, who are you to judge who is a fine fellow and who isn't? You certainly have never met me, and in fact, I have no desire to meet you. For I find you and your occupation of reading essays to be entirely despicable. I say this to shock you again, of course, and to keep your attention, for I am assured by several authorities that all essay readers work at two o'clock in the morning with a six-pack of Heineken by their side. Does my saying this offend you? Gentlemen, I assure you that it is most certainly true! In fact, speaking for myself, I would do much the same if I were in your position, but each day I offer up a thousand thanks that I am not.

But I must stop now; I may be writing too many words. Of course, the very idea of limiting a person's essay to a predetermined length is absurd, for what if that person has something to say? He should be allowed to go on considerably longer, if not indefinitely. And who should be the judge of whether a person has something important to say? I am quite confident that I have something to say, but you probably disagree with me, especially since you are well into your second six-pack by now. Well reject me then, I assure you it's all the same to me. . . . I didn't mean that, of course.

1. Copycat. No, actually, he does a decent mimicry job here and he seems to have a mind that works well.
2. Did this person intentionally sabotage his application? This is easy—deny.
3. Sounds like this kid has written too many essays using downers. Terrible strategy with obvious death wish.
4. Tedious. The attempt at creativity falls flat. Says it's all the same to him if we reject him. We needn't disappoint him. We won't miss much if the essay's any indication of what he has to offer.

Here's a classic "risk" essay—only admissions officer 1 found anything redeeming in it. And yet it is a careful and accomplished parody of Dostoevsky's *Notes from the Underground,* whose narrator is one of the most intriguingly disagreeable characters in fiction. The chance he took was that the readers might not be up on their Russian lit and might mistake the character's voice for the applicant's own (as my panelists did, in fact). But he wrote what he wanted to write, and he clearly had a good time doing it. It was also not the first parody he had ever written. Does it show enough about the writer? It shows he reads carefully and writes well (the imitation is very good), has a sense of humor, and goes his own way, though he's perhaps a little too well-defended. (Somebody on an admissions committee stood up for this guy; he was admitted Early Action from the Just Folks group to a college that takes just twenty percent of its applicants.) But three out of four admissions officers missed it. Beware: Good parodies are written by people who like to read and have a good ear for imitation. I have seen other good ones—an interview report on an applicant, supposedly written by James Joyce, comes to mind. The *real* lesson to learn from this one is that, if you are going to write a parody, the subject should not be the application process, but some other part of your life.

(F) Any topic.

In 1979 we moved to New York. Only then did I realize why I had spent the first twelve years of my life not fitting in. I was born in Tumalo, Oregon, literally a one-street town west of the Cascade Mountains in Oregon's "Dry Country." The people of Tumalo lived there because they had always lived there. Many of them didn't have the imagination or means to move.

My dad, on the other hand, did have the imagination and the means. A rebellious painter, he had fled an eastern society up-bringing for the "real-people" in Oregon and set up a studio there—a loft with white walls, wooden floors and plenty of light—where he played the guitar and painted what the townspeople called "that queer modern art." Everybody else wore a cowboy hat, plowed fields, trained horses and baled hay during the week; on weekends, they rode bucking broncoes.

My parents liked it there, but I knew early on that we weren't really part of things in Tumalo. I didn't milk a cow until my best friend, who woke to that chore every day, showed me how. I never did learn how to gather eggs or cream butter or ride horses, because I was too embarrassed to try something for the first time that all the other kids knew how to do from birth. I began to wonder why we didn't have cows to milk and horses to ride instead of books to read and oil paints and canvas to play with.

Kids need to fit in, and I did what I could. I remember strutting desperately around the rodeo grounds in my cowboy boots and jeans, happy and dusty from the powdery earth, guzzling an Orange Crush. In my memory I can still feel the cool lip of the bottle against my teeth and the sweet liquid. "At least I look like a cowgirl," I thought. A voice crackled out of the loud speaker announcing the best barrel rider and the best calf; I went over to the arena and cheered with my friend as her father came charging out of the pen on a white Palomino, right on the tail of a small black goat. I wanted *my* father to rope a goat from horseback, knock it to the ground, tie its four legs together faster than anybody else, then tip his Stetson to the crowd, spit some tobacco juice and cowboy-walk out of the arena.

I wanted more from my mother, too. It took me a long time to forgive her for my lunches. Little did she know the ordeal I went through every day with my daily cargo of ethnic foods and brown bread and organic peanut-butter sandwiches and carrots and celery; she refused to buy Wonder Bread and Twinkies. Every day in the lunchroom at Tumalo Elementary, I threw it all away without even taking it out of the bag.

My dad just wasn't going to be a cowboy, and my mother wasn't a cowboy's wife. They were Wellesley and Princeton graduates who wanted a simple life. But I don't think they realized what being different did to me. As adults, they could handle it and appreciate it. But I was the one who didn't have a heifer to enter in the 4-H competition.

I understand now what my parents wanted—the peace, the country, the howls of the coyotes at night, the absence of cocktail parties, a place where they could wear jeans and old work boots all week and didn't have to be social and send Christmas cards to business associates. I can appreciate all that now, but I was still glad when we moved to 112th Street and Broadway in a town where my friends—like me—ate souvlaki, kasha, bagels and tofu, and where modern art has a whole museum.

1. The best kind of autobiographical approach—one topic, well-covered, with a nice sense of perspective and atmosphere, providing a good feel for who the writer is.
2. I like the frustrated cowgirl. Enough spunk to make an effort and enough understanding to know why it didn't work. Interesting background. She knows herself well enough to conduct a thorough college search. She'll land on her feet. As long as she's not still annoyed with her folks, she's easy.
3. Solid essay giving some sense of the person. Quite helpful in assessing the candidate as a person.
4. Elegant, mature, and insightful essay about growing up as an outsider. *Wonderful!*

(G) *Any topic.*

There is nothing that can prepare you to meet a future stepmother. One night my dad told me he wanted to take me out to dinner with a "special friend" of his. When Dad pulled up in the car, I was surprised because dinner with Dad usually meant a walk around the corner to Al Buon Gusto for pizza or spaghetti, or sometimes to Hunan Park for egg rolls and lo mein. "Oh," I thought, standing at the curb and seeing a sweep of red hair occupying my usual seat in the Olds, "a *special* friend."

"Liz," he beamed, "THIS is EVELYN!" It was dark in the car and I couldn't see her distinctly. Just as well . . . I was embarrassed by his enthusiasm. I knew he had girlfriends, but I had never been asked to meet one before. Special Friend. "Special" buzzed through my head like a dentist's drill.

We went to a chi-chi restaurant—exposed bricks, hanging plants, sawdust on the floor. Waiting for a table, we got our first good look at each other. She was what the fashion magazines call "petite." She had tiny, delicate features, bright auburn hair in a TV starlet's coif, and ten perfectly manicured nails painted passionate pink. At six feet, I'm used to feeling taller than other women but this was ridiculous. Her painfully high heels brought her up only to my shoulder and the longer we stood waiting for a table the bigger and clumsier I felt.

I had nothing to say to her . . . to them. I slouched against the brick wall eating peanuts from the bar, avoiding small talk, and cringed when Dad abandoned us to check on our table. We tried to talk.

"Oh, look, Liz," she said. "There's sawdust on the floor; that's such a special touch. Your dad is amazing to find such a gem in this kind of neighborhood."

She oozed compliments about how "special" it was for a girl to be six feet tall. "I envy big girls like you who can just wear anything." Her compliments only made me feel more like a mountain. I wanted to sink into a hole and escape.

It felt like Dad had been gone ten years, but finally he returned and the waiter found us a table in the corner. I sat like a zombie while they tried desperately to include me in their conversation. Dad encouraged me to talk about a past summer at a tennis camp. I guess he thought that would be a subject Evelyn and I could discuss. "Evelyn is such a wonderful little tennis player," he said.

Talking to people, especially unfamiliar or difficult people, is usually stimulating, but it was a struggle with Evelyn. Maybe one reason was the way they turned their names into a rhyme—she called him "Kev," and he called her "Ev."

"Ev," I discovered over dessert, had a talent for talking, not just dressing, in clichés. Everything was "special." "This is a really special place," she would say. Or, "You're a very special person." Or, "This is such a special evening."

They got married a little over a year ago. My dad seems very happy, so since then I've been working on my tolerance. It isn't always easy. I'm their most frequent dinner guest and movie companion, but I still can't help cringing a little when I hear the word "special."

1. A sensitive handling of a difficult situation. Meeting mom's replacement can't be easy and her attitude bespeaks real maturity and poise.

2. This is painful. If the family troubles haven't upset the school work, OK. (Let's also check with the women's basketball coach. Is she really six feet tall?)

3. This essay wimped out at the end. The subject is a good one and got mostly strong treatment with good insight and humor. I like the effort, especially its human quality.

4. The discomfort of meeting father's "special" friend is effectively portrayed but gives little insight into Liz beyond that. Sounds a bit bitter, alone? Tough being a teenager.

(H) Please discuss an issue of national or international concern.

I do some of my best thinking in the bathroom. I don't mean to embarrass anyone by talking about something so private, but it's probably a good thing for you to know in case we begin a four year relationship in which I'll have to do a lot of thinking.

The reason I'm going public with this announcement is that this fall I began to see I wasn't the only one who felt inspired and peaceful in that small room where we are alone with our bodies and our thoughts. My dad, for instance, calls it the reading room. He thinks he's joking, but I noticed the bathroom is actually the *only* place he reads now. He says he's just too busy to take time for luxuries like novels. (He means in his life outside the bathroom.) My other connection was learning last year in art history class that Toulouse Lautrec, the French painter, once wanted to hang his pictures in the men's room of a restaurant so they would be fully appreciated. "It is the most contemplative moment in a man's day," he said.

I've always tried to be a good son and a good student, and so for a while I followed Dad's example and Lautrec's suggestion and passed time in the bathroom by reading or looking at pictures. But that changed one day when Mom, in a cleaning frenzy, had cleared out all the magazines and books and I wound up in there alone with the tiles and the towels. Pretty soon I got tired of reading the monograms on the face cloths and turned to the window, which looks out over a bit of lawn toward a few trees beside our house. Seated (I promise not to be crude), I wasn't thinking of anything except how bored I was. Then suddenly I was thinking of many things at once: a good opening paragraph for my history paper, a new way to look at a chemistry problem I'd been working on, even the perfect gift for my girlfriend's birthday, just to mention the more practical. I also had other thoughts rushing across my mind like clouds in a windy sky: the meaning of

long-forgotten conversations, sudden connections between very different ideas. It came out of nowhere and it was exhilarating. I felt like
a philosopher. Since then I haven't read a word in there; I just assume
the pose of Rodin's Thinker and let it happen. I guess some of it may
be just physiology (Dad says I have an "awesome metabolism"), but
there's more to it than that, a fact I learned when I once tried bringing
a pad in to make some notes; it only ruined the spell. Sometimes now
I write down what I can remember afterward, but the thinking I do
in the bathroom is pure and undistracted, and the way to do it is to
do nothing.

I get the sense from news programs I've seen that world leaders
don't spend enough time in the bathroom, let alone do much thinking there. Like my dad, they're just too busy with realities to afford
the luxury of pure reflection. As a result, I don't hear many exhilarating thoughts coming out of world leaders these days, nothing that
shows much imagination or excitement. Just the same old deadlock
on the same deadly issues. They're always flying around the world,
sending guns or warnings to one another, disrupting their digestions
and never taking the time between all those briefings to sit down and
make peace with their own biology, never mind with other countries.
Even when they're home, security reasons probably prevent them
from having bathrooms with much of a view. I bet the White House
even has a telephone in the bathroom. That would be the worst.
Maybe that's why world leaders all look so constipated, even when
they smile.

I think we'd all be better off if once a day we pumped all the heads
of state full of apple cider—Dad says it's "nature's laxative"—and
locked them for twenty minutes in small rooms with a good view of
some trees, or a hill, or a pond, or a bird's nest, away from telephones
and briefings and realities. Maybe they'd think of something.

1. In its own bizarre way this essay manages to be appealing.
    Reminiscent of Russell Baker, someone smart has started with an
    ordinary notion and played it out effectively. His wry sense of humor
    works well.
2. This is fun. He's funny. And I'd like to meet the father. All other
    things being equal, I'd want him in my class and in my dorm. Wise
    and funny, with an interesting perspective on things. He'll be
    conscientious without taking it all too seriously.
3. Good expansion of humorous subject into the verities of everyday
    life and world events. Some clever language here. A case of humor
    and self-revelation working to good end.
4. Sensitive, quite thoughtful. Some potentially crude parts in their
    graphic quality, but sincere and genuine. Does seem to be thinking.
    Good job.

And that is how to revitalize even the Miss America essay.

In every good essay, the sentences and words are simple, the thinking
vivid, the images detailed. The same can be said of the professional pieces
in the following chapter. Ultimately, you will stay on course if you keep
in mind the image of a young and otherwise energetic admissions officer
stooping like a stuffed pelican over a lump of undigested applications. It is
midnight. Wearily he opens the evening's thirty-eighth file. "I do some of
my best thinking," begins the essay, "in the bathroom." The admissions
officer smiles a little. He is restored to life.

So is the applicant.

12

ANTHOLOGY

It would probably surprise many professional reporters and editors to know that they write college essays for a living or at least dabble now and then in the form. (They have a weird idea that it's "journalism.") Look through the opinion pages and features sections of newspapers, magazines, and blogs, or in any number of small literary journals, and you'll see columns of informal, personal, and relatively short narratives that would help (if their grades and recommendations checked out) sneak them into First Choice U.

First I have a handful of recommendations for a variety of voices, followed at the end of the chapter by a few actual examples. Even if the essays are longer than 500 words, they are all up to the same thing: "The reproduction of the world that surrounds me," as the German writer Goethe wrote, "by means of the world that is in me."

You can find these in books, though almost all are available on the Internet.

CONTEMPORARIES

Nora Ephron, "A Few Words About Breasts"
bell hooks, "straightening our hair"
Chang-Rae Lee, "Coming Home Again"

Barry Lopez, "A Scary Abundance of Water" and "Madre de Dios"

Barry Lopez and Rick Bass, "On Hunting"

Nancy Mairs, "On Being a Cripple"

W. S. Merwin, "Unchopping a Tree"

Toni Morrison, "On to Disneyland and Real Unreality"

Salman Rushdie, "Out of Kansas," "An Alternative Career," "On Leavened Bread," "The Taj Mahal"

Brent Staples, "Black Men and Public Space"

Deborah Tannen, "My Mother, My Hair"

Suzanne Britt Jordan, "That Lean and Hungry Look"

CLASSICS

James Baldwin, "Stranger in the Village"

Ambrose Bierce, "Christmas and the New Year"

Zora Neale Hurston, "How It Feels to Be Colored Me"

George Orwell, "Shooting an Elephant"

Bertrand Russell, "In Praise of Idleness"

Mark Twain, "Advice to Youth"

E. B. White, "Once More to the Lake" and "Death of a Pig"

ANTHOLOGIES AND COLLECTIONS

The Art of the Personal Essay, ed. Philip Lopate

Quick Takes, ed. Elizabeth Penfield and Theodora Hill

Prose Models, ed. Gerald Levin

The Compact Reader, ed. Jane Aaron and Ellen Repetto

True Tales of American Life, ed. Paul Auster

Essays of E. B. White

The Contemporary Essay, ed. Donald Hall

Any of the Best American Essays series, which often contain personal narratives

The Norton Reader

As Yogi Berra said, "You can observe a lot just by watching." The way to get better, in writing as in baseball, is to keep your eye on the pros. Study their moves, pick up their tricks, imitate them if you like. As contradictory as it sounds, imitation is one of the quickest paths toward finding your own voice. Though he was talking about painting, the words of Pablo Picasso, the most original of artists, apply equally to writing: "You should constantly try to paint like someone else. But the thing is, you can't! You would like to. You try. But it turns out to be a botch. . . . And it's at the very moment you make a botch of it that you're yourself." In the selections below you'll hear a variety of distinctive voices. They were not written as college essays, but they could have been. That's because, although the pieces didn't "get them in" anywhere (except perhaps into our minds and hearts), they "work."

All the essays that follow could be used for the "Tell us anything you think we should know" or "Write on any topic you like" assignments. But the first three could also be responses to "Discuss a problem of national or international concern."

E. B. WHITE   *Heavier than Air*

The first time I ever saw a large, heavy airplane drop swiftly out of the sky for a landing, I thought the maneuver had an element of madness in it. I haven't changed my opinion much in thirty years. During that time, to be sure, a great many planes have dropped down and landed successfully, and the feat is now generally considered to be practicable, even natural. Anyone who, like me, professes to find something implausible in it is himself thought to be mad. The other morning, after the Convair dived into the East River, an official of the Civil Aeronautics Board said that the plane was "on course and every circumstance was normal"—a true statement, aeronautically speaking. It was one of those statements, though, that illuminate the new normalcy, and it encouraged me to examine the affair more closely, to see how far the world has drifted toward accepting the miraculous as the commonplace. Put yourself, for a moment, at the Convair's controls and let us take a look at this day's normalcy. The speed of a Convair, approaching an airport, is about a hundred and forty miles an hour, or better than two miles a minute. I don't know the weight of the plane, but let us say that it is heavier than a grand piano. There are passengers aboard. The morning is dark, drizzly. The skies they are ashen and sober. You are in the overcast. Below, visibility is half a mile. (A few minutes ago it was a mile, but things have changed rather suddenly.) If your forward speed is two miles per minute and you can see half a mile after you get out of the overcast, that means you'll be able to see what you're in for in the next fifteen seconds. At the proper moment, you break out of the overcast and, if you have normal curiosity, you look around to see what's cooking. What you see, of course, is Queens—an awful shock at any time, and on this day of rain, smoke, and shifting winds a truly staggering shock. You are close to earth now, doing two miles a minute, every circumstance is normal, and you have a fifteen-second spread between what you *can* see and what you can't. What you hope to see, of course, is Runway 22 rising gently to kiss your wheels, but, as the passenger from Bath so aptly put it, "When I felt water splashing over my feet, I knew it wasn't an airport."

Airplane design has, it seems to me, been fairly static, and designers have docilely accepted the fixed-wing plane as the sensible and natural form. Improvements have been made in it, safety devices have been added, and strict rules govern its flight. But I'd like to see plane designers start playing with ideas less rigid than those that now absorb their fancy. The curse of flight is speed. Or, rather, the curse of flight is that no opportunity exists for dawdling. And so weather is still an enormous factor in air travel. Planes encountering fog are diverted to other airports and set their passengers down hundreds of miles from where they want to be. In very bad weather, planes are not permitted to leave the ground at all. There are still plenty of people who refuse to fly simply because they don't like to proceed at two miles a minute through thick conditions. Before flight becomes what it ought to be, a new sort of plane will have to be created—perhaps a cross between a helicopter and a fixed-wing machine. Its virtue will be that its power can be used either to propel it rapidly forward or to sustain it vertically. So armed, this airplane will be able to face bad weather with equanimity, and when a pall of melancholy hangs over Queens, this plane will be seen creeping slowly down through the overcast and making a painstaking inspection of Runway 22, instead of coming in like a grand piano.

JOHN UPDIKE   *Beer Can*

This seems to be an era of gratuitous inventions and negative improvements. Consider the beer can. It was beautiful—as beautiful as the clothespin, as inevitable as the wine bottle, as dignified and reassuring as the fire hydrant. A tranquil cylinder of delightfully resonant metal, it could be opened in an instant, requiring only the application of a handy gadget freely dispensed by every grocer. Who can forget the small, symmetrical thrill of those two triangular punctures, the dainty *pffff,* the little crest of suds that foamed eagerly in the exultation of release? Now we are given, instead, a top beetling with an ugly, shmoo-shaped "tab," which, after fiercely resisting the tugging, bleeding fingers of the thirsty man, threatens his lips with a dangerous and hideous hole. However, we have discovered a way to thwart Progress, usually so unthwart-

able. *Turn the beer can upside down and open the bottom.* The bottom
is still the way the top used to be. True, this operation gives the
beer an unsettling jolt, and the sight of a consistently inverted beer
can might make people edgy, not to say queasy. But the latter difficulty could be eliminated if manufacturers would design cans that
looked the same whichever end was up, like playing cards. What
we need is Progress with an escape hatch.

RUSSELL BAKER   *Summer Beyond Wish*

A long time ago I lived in a crossroads village of northern Virginia
and during its summer enjoyed innocence and never knew boredom, although nothing of consequence happened there.

Seven houses of varying lack of distinction constituted the
community. A dirt road meandered off toward the mountain
where a bootleg still supplied whiskey to the men of the country-
side, and another dirt road ran down to the creek. My cousin Ken-
neth and I would sit on the bank and fish with earthworms. One
day we killed a copperhead which was basking on a rock nearby.
That was unusual.

The heat of the summer was mellow and produced sweet scents
which lay in the air so damp and rich you could almost taste them.
Mornings smelled of purple wisteria, afternoons of the wild roses
which tumbled over stone fences, and evenings of honeysuckle.

Even by standards of that time it was a primitive place. There
was no electricity. Roads were unpaved. In our house there was
no plumbing. The routing of summer days was shaped by these
deficiencies. Lacking electric lights, one went early to bed and rose
while the dew was still in the grass. Kerosene lamps were cleaned
and polished in an early-morning hubbub of women, and children
were sent to the spring for fresh water.

This afforded a chance to see whether the crayfish population had multiplied. Later, a trip to the outhouse would afford a chance to daydream in the Sears, Roebuck catalogue, mostly about shotguns and bicycles.

With no electricity, radio was not available for pacifying the young. One or two people did have radios that operated on mail-order batteries about the size of a present-day car battery, but these were not for children, though occasionally you might be invited in to hear "Amos 'n' Andy."

All I remember about "Amos 'n' Andy" at that time is that it was strange hearing voices come out of furniture. Much later I was advised that listening to "Amos 'n' Andy" was racist and was grateful that I hadn't heard much.

In the summer no pleasures were to be had indoors. Everything of delight occurred in the world outside. In the flowers there were hummingbirds to be seen, tiny wings fluttering so fast that the birds seemed to have no wings at all.

In the heat of midafternoon the women would draw the blinds, spread blankets on the floor for coolness and nap, while in the fields the cattle herded together in the shade of spreading trees to escape the sun. Afternoons were absolutely still, yet filled with sounds.

Bees buzzed in the clover. Far away over the fields the chug of an ancient steam-powered threshing machine could be faintly heard. Birds rustled under the tin porch of the roof.

Rising dust along the road from the mountains signaled an approaching event. A car was coming. "Car's coming," someone would say. People emerged from houses. The approaching dust was studied. Guesses were hazarded about whom it might contain.

Then—a big moment in the day—the car would cruise past.

"Who was it?"

"I didn't get a good look."

"It looked like Packy Painter to me."

"Couldn't have been Packy. Wasn't his car."

The stillness resettled itself as gently as the dust, and you could wander past the henhouse and watch a hen settle herself to perform the mystery of laying an egg. For livelier adventure there was the field that contained the bull. There, one could test his courage by seeing how far he dared venture before running back through the fence.

The men drifted back with the falling sun, steaming with heat and fatigue, and washed in tin basins with water hauled in buckets from the spring. I knew a few of their secrets, such as who kept his whiskey hidden in a mason jar behind the lime barrel, and what they were really doing when they excused themselves from the kitchen and stepped out into the orchard and stayed out there laughing too hard.

I also knew what the women felt about it, though not what they thought. Even then I could see that matters between women and men could become very difficult and, sometimes, so difficult that they spoiled the air of summer.

At sunset people sat on the porches. As dusk deepened, the lightning bugs came out to be caught and bottled. As twilight edged into night, a bat swooped across the road. I was not afraid of bats then, although I feared ghosts, which made the approach of bedtime in a room where even the kerosene lamp would quickly be doused seem terrifying.

I was even more afraid of toads and specifically of the toad which lived under the porch steps and which, everyone assured me, would, if touched, give me warts. One night I was allowed to stay up until the stars were in full command of the sky. A woman of great age was dying in the village and it was considered fit to let the children stay abroad into the night. As four of us sat there we saw a shooting star and someone said, "Make a wish."

I did not know what that meant. I didn't know anything to wish for.

ELLEN GOODMAN *A Failure of Faith in Man-Made Things*

There are those who have faith in man-made things and those who do not.

I do not.

I do not have faith in elevators. I do not have faith in planes, subways, bridges or tunnels.

I do use them. Of which fact I am very proud.

I have, for example, a friend who chose his dentist because the dentist's office was on the first floor. I know a journalist who became a national expert on trains because he can't bear flying. I have another friend who sold his island house after living there only weeks because he had dizzy spells on the bridge. (The alternative route—a tunnel—was completely out of the question.)

I don't think these people are neurotic. Rather, it's a question of degree. How many of the rest of us travel on, over and through man-made things comforted only by our private *escape* plans?

That's the dividing point. People who have faith in man-made things do not have escape plans. I do.

I have an escape plan for the elevator. I will escape Certain Death if the elevator drops twenty floors suddenly—which I fully expect—because I will be jumping up and down. I read once that if you jump up and down while the elevator is crashing you have a 50 percent chance of being up while it's down and softening the impact.

Don't tell me if it's not true.

I have an escape plan for the final subway stall. If somewhere between stops the transit line dies and there are four hundred of us squeezed into one car so tightly that no one can move an arm to break a window, I will escape. I will be at my usual post, nose in the door, gasping the one thin stream of air as it comes through a crack.

On the whole, I am more philosophical about airplanes. I look quite relaxed: seated, belted (no, I never take off my seatbelt, not even between here and Paris) and reading a paper before takeoff. I repeat ten times, "Well, it's out of my hands now." But look closer. I am in the last row, because I remember from a Jimmy Stewart movie, *The Phoenix*, that you've got the best chance of surviving near the tail. I will *escape*. If I weren't so concerned about looking cool, I would ride on the plane's rear lavatory floor.

As for bridges, I remember the Galloping Gertie. Other bridges look sturdy enough, but there is only one railing between me and the water. When I drive over them, I roll up my window, because if my car plunges into the water—it is possible, it really is—there will be an air bubble in it. I will be able to breathe until I collect myself and then execute a perfect *escape* like the ones you see on television.

Don't tell me if it isn't true.

My greatest phobia is about tunnels—maybe because my escape plans stink. Every time I go through a tunnel, I expect the Ultimate Leak. And I haven't figured any way out against the rising water except (1) drive for it or (2) run for it.

I do try to control myself. After all, I have driven through two thousand tunnels without even using the windshield wipers. But I am prepared for the worst.

I don't know how tunnels are built, or bridges, or elevators, or

airplanes. I don't know how or why they work. So why should I believe they're safe? How do I know they won't break with me on, in,
or over or under them?

My escape plans are nothing more than an attempt at control.
I know that I don't want to be dependent on the metal of a bridge,
or the concrete of a tunnel. In truth, I don't really want to depend
on man-made things at all. I hate being that far from Control Center. A severe failure of faith.

I suppose I would make one lousy astronaut.

DAVID OWEN   *Pfft*

In my mind I am seventeen, although in actual fact—in man
years—I am older. When I go to pick up babysitters, I think of
them as young contemporaries, the way eleventh-graders think of
ninth-graders. They, in contrast, think of me as a crumbling historical specimen. "I wish my dad would ever wear a jacket like
that," one of them said not long ago. She didn't mean (it turned
out) that she thought I looked sharp; she meant that she wished her
father would stop trying to dress so youthfully.

A couple of years ago in New York, I was walking down Sev-
entieth Street wearing blue jeans, sneakers, and an old sweatshirt.
Two boys in their late teens were playing football on the sidewalk.
The ball got away from them and rolled to my feet. I bent to pick it
up and toss it back. One of the boys said, "I'll get that, sir."

I am so used to being thought of as a member of the Young
Generation that the idea of becoming a member of the Old Generation is pretty hard to accept. This feeling seems to be widely
shared. Lately I have noticed that people my age usually teach their
children to address grown-ups by their first names. I am Dave or
Davey to my daughter's friends, not Mr. Owen. This may be just a

change of fashion, like the day in 1964 when my father and every other man in America stopped wearing a hat. But I think it's something else. Some of my friends don't even like to be called Mom or Dad. I can understand this. When my daughter calls me Dave, as she does occasionally, I am as thrilled as I was when I went to the front door recently and a salesman asked, "Are your parents home?"

My daughter turned two not long ago. I said to her, "Here's how old you are: One, two. Now here's how old Daddy is: One, two, three, four, five, six, seven, eight, nine, ten, eleven, twelve, thirteen, fourteen, fifteen, sixteen, seventeen [pause], eighteen, nineteen, twenty, twenty-one, twenty-two, twenty-three, twenty-four, twenty-five, twenty-six, twenty-seven, twenty-eight, twenty-nine, thirty, thirty-one." This made me feel depressed. To make myself feel better, I told her how old Grandpa is.

When my daughter was born, one of her great-grandfathers said, "I don't mind being a great-grandfather, but I can't stand being the father of a grandfather."

When I was twenty-one, I asked my father, who was fifty-one at the time, how old he felt. "Not very," he said. I asked, "How long ago does it seem since you were my age?" He thought for a moment, and then waved his hand and said, "Pfft."

13

EXHIBITS II

What follows are useful recent student examples. Each takes its own kind of risk—the risk of admitting something, not just to *get* admitted, but to discover. Although an essay of 500 words cannot (dis)cover everything, we get to know the writers well in a short space. That is the product of honest writing and conscientious revision. I've written a brief comment on each.

1.

There's a lot to be learned from a block of wood sitting on a tree stump waiting for an axe to fall, especially if the axe never makes it there and instead finds its way into your foot. As my mother frantically helped me apply gobs of Neosporin to the gash across my instep and up the base of my shin, my dad said, "Son. Study hard. Because you're definitely not cut out to be a lumberjack."

I'm proud to know a few things. I can recite the first twenty digits of pi, discuss the politics behind dueling in the nineteenth century, point out the Oedipal overtones in Act 3 Scene 5 of *Hamlet*. I could teach you the proper techniques and skills behind competitive row-ing, swimming the breaststroke, playing a riff over a D-minor chord, and saving a submerged drowning victim. I know how to cook pasta al dente, the correct way to handle a santoku, and that tomatoes and pumpkins are in fact, fruits. I even know how to unclog a toilet using Saran wrap.

But it took me an axe in my foot to drive home the realization that my knowledge at the age of seventeen isn't anywhere near complete. For every one thing I know, there are hundreds I am wholly oblivious to. The irony of an axe with a Pepto-Bismol™-pink handle nearly chopping off a few toes made me curse my naïveté. As I held the axe high above my head, right foot planted in front of left, I told myself, "I do three sports. How hard can this be?" I felt that in a second, the puny piece of lumber before me would be split cleanly in two. A second later, the only thing I felt was the axe partially embedded in my left foot. I had no understanding of the art behind wielding an axe and chopping wood. The blood dripping from the cut brought with it a barrage of questions, none of which I could answer. How often do I need a tetanus shot? How do I know if I even have tetanus? How much do prosthetic feet go for on eBay?

The large indent in my left Speedo slipper reminds me of what I learned from that axe: I don't know, and will never know everything, and always wear shoes when handling sharp outdoor equipment.

I am certainly very fortunate that my foot is in one piece. But my father's words don't ring true for me; with some practice, the expertise involved in cutting wood could be added to my bank of knowledge. Next time lumberjacks with chainsaws show up on ESPN, I'll stick to the channel to learn their trade. Just in case studying goes awry.

Small things: Notice the words instep, santoku—*the writer knows the specific names. Big things: this piece finds a personal, anecdotal way to talk about "my learning style" or "a significant learning experience," subjects that usually provoke boring, empty responses. It not only tells a story, it's aware of the story behind the story, and it holds its insight lightly.*

2.

Old cows have hairy teats, mounds of fuzzy softness that add a *woosh* to the *slurp* of the milker sliding on. Attaching the stainless steel mechanism to all four teats, however, is not always simple; the cows often stomp, whip their tails, and do evasive little Mexican Hat Dances to keep the noisy, frigid monster off their swollen udders. Soon, the barn will echo with the pump's *thump-sha-dump . . . thump-sha-dump . . . thump-sha-dump*, a steady working beat that chases the warm froth down the pipeline. At 6:00 a.m., cows aren't the happy, grass-munching frolickers milk companies like to plaster onto their cartons. They're old women in nursing homes who've been pressing down their bedside buzzers for hours, screaming "Jell-o!" at the top of their lungs.

The sun's not up yet, and the winter windows are still piled in the corner waiting to be installed, so my cold hands massaging the milk out of Mavis's massive udder probably don't feel too comforting. But the teat-washing water's extra hot today, and soaking the next towel, prepping for the dive-bomb attack it takes to scrape all the caked manure off the udder before she kicks, I have a moment to breathe. Jonathan, meanwhile, is working a few cows behind, and every once in a while he pops up from his crouch and struts down the aisle with his head thrown back, belting the refrain of Bob Dylan's "Stuck Inside of Mobile with the Memphis Blues Again," which we play over the manure-spackled speakers almost every morning. "Ohhhhh Mama, Ooooohhhhhhhhhhhh Mama!" he croons to his captive bovine audience.

Because nearly my entire life has been spent in a farming town in Wisconsin, it's ironic I never really got up-close-and-personal with a cow before my morning barn shift at The Putney School. The most popular club at DePere High is Future Farmers of America, and on Saturday evenings, most families, especially the older folks, tune in to "A Prairie Home Companion." Garrison Keillor doesn't make much up: there's a Lutheran church and a tavern on the opposite ends of almost every street, and the separation doesn't prevent the free interchange of patrons. Life in Green Bay was simple: the Packers played on Sunday, and at Saturday evening Mass the priests all prayed for a win. There was a simplicity and a rhythm to that life.

I feel it here, too, and so do the cows: at morning milking they file (usually voluntarily) into their places, seeming to know just where to go, though I doubt they can read the name tags above their stalls. Right before breakfast, we unhitch the ladies, whose udders, lightened of their burdens, swing freely. The ensuing procession to the pasture is anything but reverent, and we always have a few escape artists or older ones lagging behind to exchange friendly banter with the horses. In the afternoon, right before dinner, the whole process happens again, though usually to some "phat hip-hop," as the sun sinks below West Hill. These rhythms, of a rural life on the land, are the music that propels my day. Sometimes when I look up from under the last cow of the morning I see the giant, ruddy face of Pete, the farm manager.

"Slow down," he murmurs. "It isn't a race, you know. Talk to the cows while you milk; they'll stop kicking if you take your time."

Softly moving on, he surveys the rest of the cows filing out into the foggy Vermont morning, leaving the barn uncomfortably quiet. I pause on my way into the steamy, sour-smelling milk room. Only the sound of the small calves gathering around their water fountains remains.

What you can learn from this evocative piece: detail and how to use it. Also how observant and empathic the writer is (the way he or she feels how cold it must be for the cows), how the portrait of this new experience at a boarding school in Vermont doesn't shy away from its grosser parts—the manure everywhere, the reek of the milk. That the writer had to travel far from home to discover where he comes from—the main idea of the piece—is something beautifully implied but not stated.

3.

Organizing has very little to do with being organized. Getting people to join a union is more of a lesson in small talk and self defense. My crash course in something called "The Real World" came as I stood in front of the UW research lab, facing a door marked RESTRICTED ACCESS in slobbery spray paint, wondering what I had gotten myself into and how the hell I was going to subtly remove the wedgie my Value Village slacks had given me. I ran through the lists of scripted small talk that had been drilled into my head during my training with the Service Employees International Union, and instantaneously forgot every last amiable word as soon as the door was answered by a woman in a bio-shield rubber suit.

"Hi . . . is DianaorReneorDavidorChrisorChristheotherone here?"

"I'm Christina."

I introduced myself. "I'm from SEIU and we're . . . I mean some of your co-workers have been interested in . . ."

"Are you, by any chance, related to—?" and she named a famous folk singer.

"Not that I know of."

"Damn. I wanted his autograph."

"Well, if I was, I'd get it for you if you'd forget my horrible introduction and let me try again."

"Sure you're not related?"

"Positive."

"I'll let you start again anyway."

And so began my first conversation with a Real Live Worker. We spoke like stop-and-go traffic for twenty-five minutes, interrupted every thirty seconds by her slamming the door in my face to avoid setting off the lab's security alarm.

"So maybe I could meet you for lunch? Bring a friend if you'd like." (SLAM)

"Just so you know, I'm not very interested in joining a union."

"That's fine. Ask me questions. I just learned all the answers, so I'd be happy to share."

"I don't want you to think I'm wasting your time."

"Of course not." (SLAM)

Chris and I ate lunch while I surreptitiously pulled at my polyester pants and answered all of her questions with a fluency that surprised me more than her. But she still didn't want to sign a card authorizing SEIU to represent her. Except for working ten hours a day with disease-ridden monkeys, she said, and being paid half that of someone in a private company, she really liked her job. I gave her my brand-new snazzy phone number, printed on an even spiffier business card, and left expecting never to hear her again.

The next day she called inviting me to the monkey lab. She was ready to sign. What had changed? "My boss reprimanded me for wearing mismatched socks, which, evidently, are against dress code. A dress code which exists, evidently, for five hundred monkeys I see every day and the two humans who happen to look down at my feet. Who, evidently, are me and my boss. Who, evidently, has a stick three feet up his rear end!"

I asked her why she had worried about unions in the first place.

"I'm not interested in more money. I just want to wear mis-matched socks if I please!"

As I shuffled away with my first signed authorization card pinned tightly to the inside of my Value Village white Oxford shirt, she called after me and I turned to see Chris putting a purple sock on her left foot. "Are you sure you're not related to—?"

Starts with a nice paradox (see p. 80), and it's really just one anecdote. The writer doesn't hammer why he or she is organizing for a union; the point is not about political beliefs (they've been backgrounded) but about real-world experience. The dialogue is well done—all the excess, repetition, and false starts of the way people talk has been cut away down to the essentials, but the characters remain vivid and clear—and so, paradoxically, it does sound like natural talk.

4.

John-Michael, a french horn player from rural Georgia, and our RA, Leo, were talking about gay people. They were on the second floor of our dorm at Tanglewood, leaning on the clean white wall by my room. I was eavesdropping while composing a piece for marimba. They were talking about how seeing homosexual couples make out around camp made them uncomfortable; they also touched approvingly on the antigay Boy Scouts of America policy. ("I'm glad they have those rules.")

Drifting into the hallway, I gradually snuck myself into the conversation, asking questions and poking small, respectful holes in John-Michael's arguments. By the time he arrived at "Being gay is a sin," one or two more had entered the group. I suggested that taking the Bible word for word might be an anachronistic, primitive way to go about treating people, that in many instances—homophobia, misogyny, racism—ancient religious or cultural rules lag far behind modern morality, and that we might do better to constantly question what we do and how we think. More voices had entered; our group had expanded to a large circle, a round-robin with opinions flying across the hallway like spells in a friendly nighttime duel at Hogwarts.

I kept my composure, but I was angry at and bewildered by the persistence of ignorance and dogma. At some level I felt insulted, but at another curious; there were moments when I felt strong, and others when I felt weak. I was overwhelmed—every word I spoke was accompanied by tremulous vibrations in my chest. And in this moment of struggle and debate, I came out to fifteen or so teenage boys I had known for a week. Before my family or most of my friends knew I was gay, these boys—almost strangers—did.

The tone of the conversation immediately changed. Though after these ephemeral fifteen minutes of talk and a fleeting three weeks of playing music we would all go back to our homes and lives, I knew they saw me in a new light.

I believe that, above all, college—where I'll again be living in a dorm—should be a place where one is exposed to and deeply immersed in a mess of worldviews and ideas, and where all kinds of opinions are considered and discussed. I came out of this experience assured that I am a person who wants to know different kinds of people and ideas. I have a drive to ask questions, to stimulate important or interesting conversations, and to defend my convictions; I want to share my beliefs, talk about my passions, and learn from others. I left Tanglewood knowing that, whatever I do—be it music, science, or something else—I can contribute to a community, and to the world, by being a passionate talker and writer and an open listener. I just have to keep the conversation going.

The writer put himself on the line with intelligence and insight—and he's
actually doing with the essay, exactly what he talks about having done in the
essay—taking the chance of coming out to strangers in the interest both of facing
himself and, through the revelation of his own identity, stepping into the com-
plicated world. The coming-out essay is not uncommon, but the narrative of the
main incident here is done with skill and candor.

5.

In the sea of color I grew up in, racial consciousness was everywhere.
The only white faces were the police everyone hated, and the teachers and administrators, who didn't care if we came to class that day or
ever, since they still would be getting paid.

In elementary school, the more mixed you were, the more popular you were, because that usually meant you were lighter. The unconscious slave mentality in my community went like this: if you
were light, you were automatically a house slave, and if you were
dark, you were a field slave. Success and opportunity were reserved
for the lighter skins.

I never realized I might be light, because I was so dark compared
to all the creamfaced Puerto Ricans in my neighborhood. The West
Indians were slightly darker but had the same kinky hair, thick lips
and "bulging" eyes. To me, we were all the same, but given the way
some people made fun of my features, you would have thought I was
as dark as my mom's cast-iron skillet. Yet I was always being mistaken
for other nationalities and realized very early I could pass, today for
Cuban, tomorrow Guyanese.

In junior high (The Special Music School), I was one of the few colored anything. All around me were Russian Jews, Russian Catholics,
Ukrainians and a large percentage of what I thought of as "the usual
white USA folk." I, along with five other students of color, would

either be ostracized or admired for our skin. This was a time when my confidence grew, because even though I was light they considered me dark and wanted to be just like me: "black." Maybe they thought it was cool. For the students who did not want any part of blackness, their racist remarks or actions made my *guess-what-happened-today-at-school-mamma?* conversations very interesting when I arrived home to 172nd Street. I would try to tell my friends on the block about the insults I endured, but before I could finish my sentence, someone would interrupt, "What does it matter, you light skinned anyways . . . you just like them." This was the first time I realized I was also different from my dark-skinned brethren. I was the person they hated but at the same time the lightface they strove to be. I became an enemy in my own neighborhood because they could not get close to the real enemy.

In 1712 a British West Indian named Willie Lynch was invited to Virginia to give a speech to other slave holders on "how to keep a slave." To promote loyalty and devotion in slaves, he suggested dividing the young and the old, the men and the women, and, significantly, light- and dark-skinned. Long afterward, cut up into small groups, people of color have struggled to find commonality. My African-American *sistren* would tease me for my light skin and then envy me because I supposedly "had it easy." I didn't see what they saw, because I knew more about our erased history than some other African-American children. In my eyes we were all in the same boat, with a hole in the side and water pouring in.

So I would argue for hours that I was not light skinned, and we would put our arms next to each other in a game I could never win. I didn't know what to say, so I didn't say anything at all. I would just wait until three o clock, when the sun was still high in the sky, and stand underneath and soak it in.

A fierce voice here, and a great open ending that resists an easy moral or a packaged sentiment. One of many risks in this is the edginess of that voice. Note the brilliant "jump" transition to paragraph five—it can't be done better, and the paragraph that follows shows an excellent use of background knowledge or research. It's worth learning the knack of making those associative leaps that seem to be a change of direction but actually deepen the idea that's already in play. In putting racial identity front and center of the "who am I?" question, the essay earns that risk through its detail and tough-mindedness.

6.

I am a terrible dancer. As everyone in my family knows, my dancing is more Abbott and Costello than Astaire and Rogers. There are at least three problems.

Rhythm

In eighth grade, like everyone else, I obsessed over the final dance in *High School Musical,* practicing the choreography with my friends. Try as I did to shimmy and rock, my arms and legs seemed to run on their own circuits. My dad used the word "asynchronous."

Agility

In fencing, the unpredictable rhythms of my lanky arms are assets, enabling foil extension in surprise ripostes. In the chem lab, which often requires careful handling of potent acids in exact volumes, I have never spilled a drop. But turn on the music and I'm more likely to turn an ankle than turn funky.

Once, as bridesmaid at a cousin's wedding, with a string quartet playing Bach's *Air on G String,* I was supposed to glide down the aisle. Lifting the train of my chiffon gown, I tried to match my steps to the ethereal music, and I might even have reached the altar if I hadn't stumbled over my hem and careened into seated guests.

Coordination

After some exciting but unsuccessful auditions, in my junior year I was thrilled to land my first part, a "best friend" role in a small independent film. A few weeks before shooting, when I got the script, one scene leapt to my eyes.

Interior. Nighttime. A prom. Music is loud and raucous. A dance floor is packed with gyrating kids.

Wait. Dance floor?

The dance moves are overtly sensual, charged, and athletic. A couple is dancing, working up a sweat together.

Oh dear. As I obsessively practiced my best moves at home, my brother could not stop laughing. It's one thing to dance in front of your family. It's quite another to have your stumbles preserved on film. When the moment came on set, while the crew adjusted lighting and marks, the actor playing my date said, helpfully: "Don't worry, you'll get used to it."

Get used to what? "They film the dancing without music." I stared at him. I must have uttered something unintelligible, because he smiled and clarified, "They'll edit the music in at the studio." To prepare, I had been practicing to the driving rhythm of the exact song named in the script. Now, not only did I have to be filmed dancing, but I also had to do it *without music.*

When I came out of my trance, the director called action; the only sound was the staccato clacking of shoes as we started. My left ankle wobbled in my platform heels. Thankfully, my partner was graceful and skilled. He steadied me with his arm while continuing to move fluidly.

As any bad dancer knows, dancing in public can be embarrassing. Dancing in public with cameras trained on your every move and no music is . . . unforgettable. After a take, the director stepped out. "I want you to slink around each other and really move," he instructed us, bopping, swiveling, and jiggling to demonstrate. I was impressed. A balding man in his late fifties, he danced more skillfully than I ever could. Maybe the absence of music could be a blessing. In the next take I swung my arms in the air and shook and shimmied with what I hoped was gusto. Who knows what the rhythm was? Even though my heels stomped on my poor partner's feet, we laughed and kept on. We began to move to our own rhythms, natural in his case, "asynchronous" in mine. I couldn't stop smiling.

After the director shouted cut, my partner gave me a thumbs up. I returned his gesture. Was he kidding? "You guys had great chemistry together," trumpeted the director. "It looks fantastic on camera!"

I don't know about Ginger Rogers, but I thought Abbott and Costello would approve.

This is a very engaging approach to something most students (and all parents and counselors) are terrified of—the something-I'm-really-bad-at essay. I don't mean to make it sound like it's a genre—would that it were. If you're ever stuck for an essay topic, try it; my experience in the classroom with students is that if they give themselves to it, undefensively, they usually write terrific pieces. Your parents and counselors may think you've lost your mind to be focusing so much on a flaw, and a seemingly trivial one at that. Yet this piece shows how the flaw can be used to reveal a passion and an achievement.

7.

"Not today." I had said those words hundreds of times to sidewalk fund-raisers, but always with eye contact and a smile. On this day in June, though, I focused straight ahead and definitely did not smile.

I was walking home from my internship at Memorial Sloan-Kettering Cancer Center when a woman with a clipboard corralled me and asked, "Do you have a moment for animal rights?" On any other day, I would have slipped comfortably into my busy New Yorker mode. But on this day, for the first time, I meant my well-rehearsed two-word salutation literally.

A few hours earlier I had "sacrificed" my first lab animal. A post-doctoral candidate working at the lab had asked me to assist her with some research on amyotrophic lateral sclerosis. One of the rat models had lost motor function and would not live much longer; we had little choice but to put it down. My mom was nervous for me when she found out we worked with live rats because I have always loved animals and constantly pestered her to allow me to adopt a shelter dog. On the street that day, I felt the guilt my mom had been trying to protect me from. I was not ashamed of what I had done, but the coincidence was disconcerting.

This past summer at the lab, I worked mainly on the Radiation Project. The experiment focused on using stem cells to repair cognitive damage from radiation therapy administered to postoperative pediatric cancer patients. We radiated the brains of young rats and then injected them with specially treated human embryonic stem cells. Because I had spent the previous summer mastering the necessary techniques, I was given full responsibility to section, stain, and collect data from two radiated brains into which we had transplanted stem cell grafts. Although I rarely worked directly with living rats, I was always conscious that the tissue I was handling came from living beings. But whenever I doubted my work, I would think of another coincidence in my life that easily trumped my street-side encounter.

When I was younger, my uncle had a big bald spot he attempted to cover with what seemed to me a pitiable ponytail. I knew it had something to do with a brain tumor, but it was not until I described the lab's stem cell experiment to my father that I learned the bald spot was a direct result of radiation. When my uncle was still in elementary school, he was diagnosed with malignant brain cancer. No one in our family thought he would live; imaging tools like MRIs were not yet available, and the "blind" surgery was very risky. But thanks to a fantastic surgeon and postoperative radiation, he survived with only mild cognitive deficiencies. My uncle was lucky that the collateral damage from the radiation therapy was not more debilitating. Even today, many such children are not so fortunate.

My fascination with neural stem cells would have been motivation enough, but the realization that my research could have helped somebody close to me solidified my drive. Then one day, during my last week at the lab, I looked at one of my rat brain sections under the microscope and saw red fluorescence in a human stem cell graft. I ran to my supervisor. As she looked down at the slide, her smile widened, and I knew I had found what the lab had spent many years searching for. Those few red cells with elongated morphologies were incorporating into the rat brain and replacing the cells destroyed by radiation. The head of the lab made a special trip to my team's microscope to view my slide and confirm our first positive result. Within the brain of a rat, the brain that I had prepared and evaluated, was my small contribution to the future of pediatric radiation therapy.

Since then I have not yet encountered an animal rights advocate with a clipboard. When I do, though, I plan on stopping and having a conversation. I do not know where it will lead, but I feel much better prepared.

Frank and moving exploration of what is elsewhere often vaguely referred to as "values." Happily, the word itself never appears. Here we get to see the writer making sense of her day-to-day life. A side benefit is the rejuvenation of the lab work essay—and also of the success essay, usually so dreary. But remember: You don't have to have a breakthrough to make a lab essay work—you just have to observe details carefully, be very specific, and reason closely from the evidence— just like good lab work, come to think of it.

8.

I remember exactly what I was wearing the first day of ninth grade when I walked through the Plexiglas door of the lobby of the Shipley Upper School: a black fitted T-shirt from the women's section of American Eagle, corduroy shorts that just barely passed the extend-at-least-as-far-as-the-fingertips-of-the-wearer-when-her-arms-are-at-her-sides dress code of the prestigious private day school in Bryn Mawr. Birkenstocks and my plain brown hair parted down the middle, in a ponytail at the nape of my neck: the hairstyle and clothing of a girl caught in her own skin. But now if you tried to find a trace of Tracey, the shy girl who did an excellent job of blending in, you'd come across a shadow. You won't see my senior page at the end of the L section in the yearbook, though my name might be scribbled on the "Gone, But Not Forgotten" tribute to former classmates in the back.

You'd get the same sense of something missing if you tried to find pictures of little Adam in the cub scouts, or in a suit and a clip-on tie at his Grandparent's fiftieth anniversary. But he was there. Xeno's paradox states that if something travels between point A and B, theoretically the distance keeps halving itself, and you will never reach point B because the distance of one half gets infinitely smaller. This is true about my life—I will never reach that boundary line between Tracey and Adam. Tracey wasn't a girl, and Adam isn't a boy—I'm lost somewhere halfway between point A and point B. Last spring I sat in the headmaster's office and stated that it would be absurd to put a flat-chested boy who needs to shave his chin stubble in a girl's dorm again. He and the rest of the staff were flustered by this dilemma; "I'm sorry, but your anatomy does not qualify you to live in a boy's dorm—you must understand that this is an issue of legality and safety." I've held off from getting a driver's learning permit or license until I get my name and gender legally changed—I'm too scared of the scenario that might ensue if a police officer pulls me over and compares TRACEY LEWIS/FEMALE with the driver he's looking at. I don't want to face his confusion or disbelief, and I do not want to end up explaining my life story to a cop when the only real problem is that one tail light was out.

It's simple enough if you look up the definition of a transsexual. My body was born female, and because of that, I was raised in society as a female, to believe that I am female. However, I am not a female—a realization that I made after spending long hours of research when I was fifteen. This summer I underwent chest reconstruction surgery and started taking testosterone injections to help align my body chemistry with my brain chemistry. But if the whole process were that straightforward, maybe I'd be "normal" and happy with people's assurance that they see me as "just a normal guy." Maybe then you could slap a label on me and call it finished.

I say that I am male when I don't have the time or patience to explain the complexity of my gender, because it is the closest I can come to explaining myself in the limited language that our society offers. But I'm not "normal," nor am I a male. I'm a boy who isn't allowed to live in a boy's dorm. I'm a guy with a voice that didn't start to change until I was seventeen. I'm only now learning how to be "one of the guys." I had to teach myself how to tie a tie, and my first haircut was at age fifteen, not two. You would not find my anatomy anywhere in even the most advanced textbook; I am an XX man.

I sit on the line between boy and girl. I'm not point B—I'm half of a half of a half of the distance of someone traveling from point A to point B; I'm caught somewhere in infinity. But I like sitting in-between—it allows me to see the world from a perspective that no one from either end could see.

Not everyone will have such dramatic material to work with. But it's a good example of how to represent the risk of a major self discovery in a brief essay. This was written by one of the bravest students I've ever known, and the essay is a testament to that courage, written with intelligence and even wit—the use of Zeno's paradox is an inspired moment of metaphor, and of projecting the self into seemingly dry schoolwork or research and making it burn with purpose.

25TH ANNIVERSARY EDITION

What does an admissions officer look for in a college application essay?

You. It's that simple. There's no formula, no trick, no strategy, says Harry Bauld, a former Ivy League admissions officer. But with acceptance rates at all-time lows, just being yourself in an essay means understanding your readers and the unique form in which you are writing. In this fully revised and updated edition of the classic guide to writing the best essay of your life, Bauld reveals the big clichés (The Trip, The Jock, Miss America, Pet Death) and helps you discover ways to come alive on the page as a real person instead of applicant number 13,791.

HARRY BAULD has been a writer, teacher, and speaker for thirty years. He has worked in admissions and college counseling at high schools and universities, including Brown and Columbia, and is currently an English teacher at Horace Mann School in New York.

Cover design by Anthony Morais

COLLINS REFERENCE

Visit www.AuthorTracker.com for exclusive information on your favorite HarperCollins authors.

Study Aids/General

ISBN 978-0-06-212399-2

USA $14.99